An advanced fishing guide
for the largemouth bass

The
Bass
Angler

John R. Jeffries

Badger Books Inc.

© Copyright 1996 by John R. Jeffries
Published by Badger Books Inc. of Oregon, Wis.
Illustrations by John R. Jeffries
Editing/proofreading by J. Allen Kirsch
Cover color separations by Port to Print of Madison, Wis.
Printed by BookCrafters of Chelsea, Mich.

ISBN 1-878569-35-X

Publishers Cataloging in Publication
(Prepared by Quality Books Inc.)

Jeffries, John R.
    The bass angler : an advanced fishing guide to the largemouth bass / John R. Jefferies
    p. cm.
    ISBN 1-878569-35-X

    1. Largemouth bass fishing. 2. Largemouth bass. I. Title.
SH681.J44 1996   799.1'7'58
                           QB196-20017

To Paula M. Jeffries
1948 - 1993
Who taught us all that life is not a bowl
of chocolate pudding

The beauty within nature and its com-
plexities that we just assume serve only
one purpose:
survival

Author's Note

This book is directed to all who are ready to take a serious look at this most incredible fish, the largemouth bass. You may agree or disagree with some of my findings but throughout this book is the spirit of my research and relationship to this most notable quarry.

Contents

1. INTRODUCTION

S ince my youth I have been looking for rationalizations of why bass do what they do and how it relates to me as an angler. I've come to the realization that I can not understand the bass totally, primarily because I am not a bass, nor do I pretend to live my life surrounded by bass. I can only describe to you what I have seen or experienced when I have been fishing for bass or diving in the waters they call home.

There have been numerous books, magazine articles, television and even radio discussions on just about everything you can imagine when it comes down to the life of this critter we call the largemouth bass. In this book I will present to the reader a fresh distillation or explanation of my research into the world of the largemouth bass.

From the factual standpoint it is hard for many people to understand why anyone would want to get up at four in the morning just to go after some slimy creature that Mother Nature deliberately gave a smaller brain, but finds a way to outwit most humans.

In reality, most of the cunning that we attribute to the largemouth actually stems from our own stupidity. A friend once told me that the reason we find it hard to understand bass is, "He's a full-time bass, and for the most part we're just part-time anglers." So, before we try to understand the bass, let's have a look at ourselves first as part-time anglers.

2 THE ANGLER

When it comes down to fishing psychology we all have our reasons for being out in pursuit of the largemouth bass. Whether we are tournament anglers or out looking for the catch of the day, we justify our actions for being out there simply because we enjoy the thrill of the hunt and the feeling of success.

Success can come in many forms, and it may not always be the biggest bass. For the child that may be out there for the first time, it may be that little bluegill that Grandpa or Grandma helped land, while to the tournament angler it may be first place among his or her peers. No matter who we are, the feeling of being successful feels good, while not being successful just plain feels bad. Even as simplistic as that may sound, you would be surprised at how many people don't take the time to prepare for success.

We have all seen the guy who will go out and buy a new boat along with hundreds of lures and other contraptions, then go out in the middle of a lake that he has never seen before, hoping that he'll catch some type of fish.

This is the type of guy who will come back to the dock and blame his not catching anything on everything but himself. The problem with this scenario is that it occurs much too often for the sake of saving face. Some people are under the illusion that success is something that they deserve and not something at which they must work.

No matter what type of angling you are into, whether you are a competitive angler or a meditative angler, one of the keys to success is to be able to grow in knowledge about your particular type or style of fishing.

Learning a particular behavior or trait of any fish may give you a means of predicting and adjusting to the fish's actions on any given day. All living forms repeat certain acts that enable them to adapt to their ever-changing environment. Unfortunately, most anglers expect the fish to conform to their needs and acclimate itself to their environment. We see this variety of angler often frustrated and making excuses that accompany his or her lack of success.

Sometimes we'll see an angler that has become what I call a perpetual procrastinator. They're the ones that keep putting off learning about different aspects of fishing just so they can make up something to throw you off track or tell you about the one they just missed because something was wrong with the fish, the weather, the water or whatever.

I have made a small list of excuses sometimes used by the perpetual procrastinator. Do any sound familiar?

pH WRONG.
WATER IS TOO WARM.
WATER IS TOO COLD.
FISH NOT BITING.
TOO MANY WEEDS.
WRONG BAIT.
WATER TOO DEEP.
WATER NOT DEEP ENOUGH.
WATER TOO CHOPPY.
WIND IS WRONG.
RAIN.
AIN'T NO FISH IN LAKE.
TOO EARLY IN DAY.
TOO LATE IN DAY.
BAD BOTTOM.
FISH COULD SEE LINE.
FISH COULD SMELL ME.
WRONG COLORS.

The list could go on and on, and I'm sure you have a few that you have heard yourself, and even though some of these excuses could be a genuine factor, it does not vindicate anyone for an apparent lack of knowledge.

3. IDENTIFICATION

"**W**hy is it important that we know about the largemouth bass? Why can't we just go out and catch him?" You would be surprised how many times I'm asked those questions, and my answer is, "Yes, you could just go out and catch him," and it's true anyone could, given a little bit of luck and the right day.

The real distinction among anglers is the consistency with which they are able to catch large bass in all conditions. To do this with any coherence, one must know the adversary.

The largemouth bass belongs to the sunfish family, *Centrarchidae,* and at one time was thought to belong to the perch family, but because of the technological and research advancements in the field of species identification, was transferred by the biologists to the sunfish family. The largemouth was even looked upon in early times as a trash fish that lived in the muck and mire of the shallows, not worthy of a true angler's hook. It wasn't until the 1800s that this overly large mandible swamp fish began to become popular among the fishing society.

Because of the bass' distinctive aggressive behavior, its popularity rose quickly, and it is now one of the most sought-after game fish in the United States today. It can be found virtually in every state except Alaska, as far north as Canada and as far south as Mexico. The largemouth bass has even been successfully planted in Japan and is sought after as a distinguished trophy.

THE LARGEMOUTH BASS

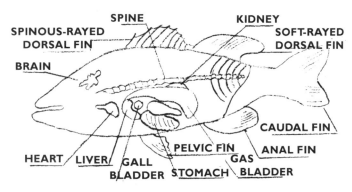

Here in Wisconsin, we have a good population of largemouth and because of the abundance of other good game fish, overfishing is not of any great concern. Due to environmental changes in many Wisconsin lakes, we should be put on notice that all game fish within our borders are in jeopardy of decline.

As a young boy I remember fishing in Lake Ripley, Wisconsin. Back then, there was an ideal bass structure that surrounded the entire lake. Now, there is less than 20 percent of good shore structure in comparison. Lake Ripley currently holds the Wisconsin largemouth bass record at 11 lbs. 13 oz., taken back in 1940. It's a record that needs to be broken.

When it comes to fish having smarts, the largemouth bass gets an A+. It is one of Wisconsin's shrewdest, having the ability to quickly learn and adapt to its changing circumstances.

Largemouth bass, as with all fish, operate on a very primitive positive or negative input sequence as a mode for learning particular survival patterns. Big bass become big bass because they make few mistakes that jeopardize their life.

One aspect of the largemouth's survival patterns that we, as anglers, can take advantage of is its feeding response. Largemouth bass are very aggressive by nature, and triggering a positive feeding mode could depend upon our presentation, but we should remember that bass are not always in a high state of feeding obsession, and triggering an attack-and-consume response could take a little finesse.

Bass don't have a sense of being full while eating. Therefore, feeding is more environmental than it is an actual thought process. In fact, as long as the environmental circumstances are in its favor, it will continue to eat until it can no longer swallow. So any of the dock talk that you hear, such as, "A bass will go to a warmer spot when it has a full belly to relax," might be questioned. It is most likely going to a different location because environmental conditions have changed and now the bass must be imposed upon to relocate, not because it has a full belly. (For more on digestion, see Chapter 15.)

For identification purposes, *Micropterus Salmoides*, or old bucket mouth, starts out life looking somewhat like a small cigar with fins. As it gets older, the overall girth becomes wider while its body becomes longer. The dorsal fin found on its back can be divided into two different parts. The anterior dorsal fin generally has ten elongated, sharp spikes that rise above an extended membrane, and the posterior dorsal fin has thirteen softer, elongated spikes within a smooth curvilinear membrane that extends back over a portion of the tail section (see diagram on page 13). The caudal, or tail, fin is well-rounded at the tips with softer spikes surrounded by a flexible membrane and is able to exhibit a fan-like display.

One of the more recognizable aspects of bass identification is it most obvious feature: its large mouth. The upper jaw plate on the largemouth extends back just beyond its copper-tone colored eye. The copper-tone colored eye is another good identifying characteristic.

When it comes to the color of the largemouth bass, you may see some variations of tones depending on the turbidity of the waters. Basically they will have dark green on their backs, with lighter green on their sides. As you look toward the belly, it will turn from a very light green to almost white in appearance at the very bottom (pigmentation will be re-examined in a later chapter). On its sides, there will be speckling of black dabs that run from the eye to the caudal fin.

In the early stages of its life, the bass appear lighter in color with more distinct coloration marks. As the largemouth becomes older, its distinct color patters start to blend and are subjected to change in contrast with the surrounding environment.

Bob, an old fishing buddy of mine, and I once took a bass to a taxidermist and without hesitation he told us from which lake it had come.

He was able to do this because the surrounding lakes gave each of the bass a unique coloring he was able to recognize. Later, when Bob and I picked up the fish, it was a true lifelike rendition of not only the fish, but also the lake's effect upon the fish's color.

Mother Nature has made sure that the largemouth bass is unequaled for its particular territory, and after years of genetic acclimation, it is truly a master of its habitat.

4. LOCOMOTION

It is very obvious to us all that fish are not all built alike and, for good reason, as they all must fit in their own ecological niche in life's master plan. In order for Mother Nature to regulate the population of all species, she devised the rule of survival. To exist, one must be able to live either within a group or be able to persevere outside of a particular group. When a fish is not effective within a particular survival pattern, its life is in jeopardy.

Not all vulnerable fish live in a certain area of a lake or stream, nor do they live in the same ecological area. Because of this, predator fish have developed their own body styles to accommodate moving about in these areas in order to feed.

One of the most visual observations that we are able to make when it comes to carangiform locomotion (see glossary, page 125) is the placement and style of the fins upon a fish. On the largemouth bass, the anterior dorsal fin assists the fish during aggressive, slow maneuvering in the prevention of pitching side to side, acting somewhat like a flecking on an arrow. The posterior dorsal fin not only aids in keeping the fish upright, but also assists in stopping. During very aggressive fast flight, the fins may fold down to lessen the drag. Some fins and the way they are displayed are also thought to help in the communication among fish. An anterior dorsal fin that is upright may help other fish to identify a bass that is in a active mode and make the prey fish more cautious in getting too close.

The pectoral fins assist the bass in many ways when maneuvering about. Extended, they can be positioned to act as a diving or surfacing rudder depending on the amount of angle or pitch. If one fin is retracted, the opposing fin acts as a pivotal drag, forcing a turn to that side. If both fins are used in a back sweeping action, it will enable the bass to move backwards and, when fully expanded out to the side position, the bass is able to stop its forward progress.

The pelvic fins help in the abdominal alignment and, since the largemouth's eyes are more suited for seeing above its body rather than below, the pelvic fins also help the bass to acclimate itself in association to the bottom by gently touching or brushing against it. In doing so, this helps to protect its soft underside where even the smallest of scratches on it could put it at risk for an infection and death. The anal fin also helps with body positioning and in stopping forward motion.

The caudal fin is the largest of the fins on a bass and plays a major role in locomotion. Of equal size on both the dorsal and ventral sides (isocercal), the caudal fin provides the bass with a concentrated thrust enabling it to charge forward surprising its prey, or it can provide a slow methodical rhythm when in a nonaggressive mode. The same slow, efficient rhythm can also be used as it approaches an unsuspecting meal. The caudal fin is also very important at spawning time, when the male uses it to fan an area, clearing it of loose debris in order to create a nest. (See Chapter 17.)

As you can see, all the fins work as a unit of balance and counterbalance, making locomotion possible. Since the fins are positioned more evenly over its entire body, unlike that of a northern pike, the bass can maneuver into position to strike at even the most inconsistent lure characteristics.

If we were to look at the bass in slow motion as it is moving through the water, we would notice a wave-like motion that starts towards the head and works its way back to the caudal fin. This is caused by the systematic firing of impulses that trigger each of the small muscle fibers that are located along the entire length of its body. Sometimes a bass will intentionally hold in a flexed side wave configuration for maximum bolting speed in anticipation of a strike. This is an offensive lunge posture.

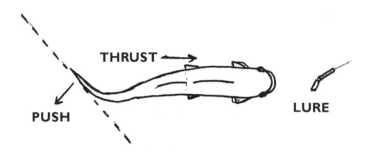

THRUST

PUSH

LURE

The bass is a white-muscled fish and isn't known for its endurance when it comes to long-distance high-speed swimming. For short distances, its powerful drive is unsurpassed and has been an important part of many bass anglers' reasons to weather bad waters so they can experience such strength.

Although a bass is able to flex its body in a side wave type of configuration, it has very little movement when it comes to bending in an upward and downward motion. The inability to accomplish this particular movement leaves it in a strange predicament when it is close to the surface and needs to go back to deeper water. In order to correct this problem, the bass must roll to its side and assume a position that will enable it to descend, a movement called side-flex rotation. Because the side-flex rotation offers the best defensive posture and the most resistance, as well as thrust potential, you often see this particular movement just after a surface strike on a lure or as you try to bring a bass to the surface.

The swim bladder, or air bladder, also plays a role in the ability of a fish to maintain stability and buoyancy within the water and assists in the overall performance of locomotion. Water is less dense than a bass and, like a rock thrown into water, a bass would also sink if it were not equipped with special adaptations such as the swim bladder. Because the bass depends heavily upon the ability to hover at a certain depth, the swim bladder plays a vital role in its existence. By using the swim bladder, less energy is consumed by the fins for hovering.

Not all fish have swim bladders. Some of the fish that forage off the bottom have no need for the ability to hover over weeds or other structures and, likewise, not all swim bladders are located in the same anatomical position as in other fish. In the largemouth bass, it is located close to its midpoint to aid in balance.

Action of the gills also aid in the movement of the bass but to a much lesser degree. As water is taken in through a bass' mouth, it is ejected towards the back of the fish, causing a small amount of propulsion and forcing the bass forward. This particular action is usually counterbalanced by a gentle back-sweeping motion of the pectoral fins.

How fast do bass swim? A general rule of thumb is to take the total length of the fish and divide it by 1.75. A bass with a length of 14 inches would swim about eight mph but may obtain flight speeds of 12 mph for a short distance.

To get an approximate flight speed, you can use the following formula:

(L) div. by 1.75 = (SP) div. by 2 = (   ) + (SP) = (FLSP)

        L = length
        SP = speed
        FLSP = flight speed

5. VISION

For years there were often many arguments when it came down to what people thought largemouth bass were able to see. Only in recent times have we been able to better understand the complex integration of its visual world through electronic diagnostic evaluation and even with this technology we can only guess its perceptible world.

Before we get into the actual structural aspects of the bass eye, I think we should take a look at light and its significance. Illumination is an essential ingredient in the bass world. The light can be direct or indirect but its importance in the daily activities of a bass is of great consequence.

Light reacts differently when passing through water than it does when passing through air. The absorption of a particular wavelength in water will vary throughout the spectrum. The wider the wavelength, the less it is able to penetrate the deeper depths. The red wavelength is the first to go, turning almost black in as little as ten feet of water. Orange is the next, followed by yellow then green and blue. Color values will vary with water clarity.

Bass that have adapted to a zone one or zone two environment or littoral zone (close to shore) will use a wider visual range when it comes to color identification when in search of prey. Although they may react more aggressively to a specific color, their strike color preference may be within a wide range of tones or hues.

Because most waters differ in the degree of clarity, the actual amount of light penetration will vary a great deal. Furthermore, there may be a certain amount of turbulence that may alter the wavelength's ability to penetrate to any particular depth. To assume that a fish is striking a particular lure only because of its color may not be entirely correct because other factors come into play.

As a lure moves through the water, it is continually undergoing color changes because it is constantly shifting in its depth, angle and water clarity. As a fish approaches the lure for a possible strike, the distance between the fish and lure obviously shortens, changing the amount of light reflection off the lure. The total color change will depend on its distance when the fish first surveyed the lure. This is good reason for the angler to follow through with a particular colored lure at the same depth of an earlier strike.

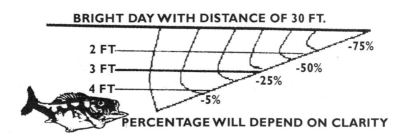

BRIGHT DAY WITH DISTANCE OF 30 FT.

2 FT — -75%
3 FT — -50%
4 FT — -25%
-5%

PERCENTAGE WILL DEPEND ON CLARITY

Since fish do not have a sense of being full after eating, successful predator fish will eat when two things happen: first, opportunity, and second, natural cycles. Light falls into the second category. Because the earth goes through day and night cycles, much of the prey will react within given light intensities throughout the 24-hour cycle to maintain their own existence. When these prey activities increase to a point at which they become a visual stimulus, especially for shallow-water bass, an innate releasing mechanism (I.R.M.) helps to trigger bass into a strike-and-consume situation.

Bass are able to distinguish light variations through I.R.Ms (more on I.R.Ms in Chapter 16) that produce the chemical change that stimulates an active feeding response. It is significant to us as anglers to predict the same light changes in order to take advantage of these ideal or peak feeding times.

It's important not only to choose a lure because of its close appearance and action to a natural prey within any portioned water, but also to pay attention to color contrast, light values of lures and how they may stand out against a given background.

Light may also affect the physical development rate of the bass. In Wisconsin, the duration of sunlight exerts a great deal of influence on thyroid activity, which increases the bass' activity. Since more energy is extended towards the consumption of food, more of the surplus energy is able to be utilized for growth and development.

The bass eye is able to differentiate somewhere between 20 to 30 color variations, depending on its environmental exposure to some or all color possibilities. It is believed that bass perceive colors much as humans perceive colors. This assumption is based on the fact that, like us, bass eyes consist of rods and cones.

Rods permit the bass to perceive black, white and shades of gray while the cones enable it to discriminate colors. As the day gradually becomes brighter, the rods very slowly retract, letting the cones differentiate colors. In a low-light situation, the rods move slowly forward and allow the bass to distinguish objects in a lower degree of illumination.

Because the bass is primarily a sight feeder, anglers may want to remember to use more blacks, whites and grays at night in order to take advantage of the rods' capability of distinguishing in lower-light conditions. On top of the water, where silhouettes will be most likely seen, black is an ideal color of choice. Just the opposite can be said for fishing on a nice sunny day. Cones are able to evaluate colorants in brighter conditions, so full vivid colors with some small patches of black or white would be the best lure for zone one or two fishing.

Each cone has the capability of discerning a particular color, with red as the most prominent followed by green and orange. Yellow and blue seem to be the hardest to detect for the bass, appearing almost black.

These color formats do pose a couple of questions. Why is it that the colors that bass respond to seem to conflict with those colors most easily seen in water? Since green is a combination of yellow and blue, why is green higher on the list than yellow or blue in colors recognized by the bass? We should remember that each cone is free from the influence of other cones and, over the course of time, develops a recognizable color range closest to its prey's colors.

Red is possibly the most recognizable because of the coloration of the gills on other fish, which presents a clear head attack for the bass. It also could indicate a fish in distress that is bleeding. I favor a little red on all of the top-water lures I use.

The shape of the bass eye leads us to believe that it is near-sighted but recent studies have indicated that bass are able to focus on objects much farther away than previously thought. Although it may be able to pull the lens back to assist in focusing at shorter distances, very long-range focusing is doubtful. A bass' perceptive vision may be only as far away as three feet. While some objects may be noticeable as far away as 30 feet, it is questionable that they appear very distinct. Water clarity is a primary factor here.

When visibility is at question, a larger lure with obvious color configurations may be the key to promoting a top-water strike, since its overall motion is more detectable.

In the underwater world of the largemouth bass, food or foe can approach from all directions. This is why it is important for the bass to have a large field of vision. Horizontally, bass have the capability of seeing 170-180 degrees while, by comparison humans see about 150 degrees.

In the vertical field, its range of vision is

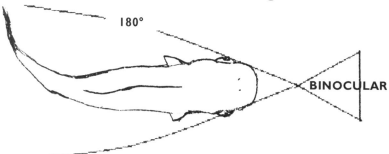

BINOCULAR VISION IS LIMITED TO A VERY SHORT RANGE

around 150 degrees while humans reach about 130 degrees. Unlike human vision, which has 120 degrees of binocular vision (able to see depth), much of the bass' vision is monocular, encompassing only 20-30 degrees of binocular vision. Although the bass may see more clearly in its forward view, it is better suited for long-sighted vision laterally.

Because bass have such a large field of vision, it's imperative that the angler be as inconspicuous as possible when moving into a bass area. Keep as low of a profile as you can and your body movements to the minimum.

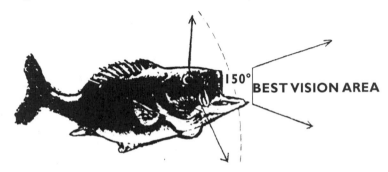

One unique physical characteristic of light and water that the bass can visually take advantage of, is the water's capacity to refract. Objects above the surface are capable of being seen at a lesser angle. Because the object within the angle occupies the higher levels of the viewpoints, it will be more readily detected. As the bass descends, the angle becomes less of an advantage. Due to this attribute, objects that would not usually be seen and could put the bass in jeopardy, are recognized as a possible threat, enabling the bass to take flight.

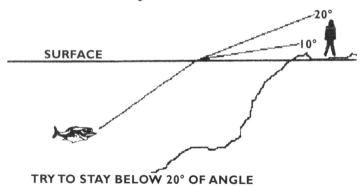

TRY TO STAY BELOW 20° OF ANGLE

Much of the bass' ability to observe its environment depends on the water condition and clarity. On those days that the water is rough, light diffuses differently than on calm days, making visual confirmation difficult. On those days, I prefer using larger lures that have wide bands of visible color and a snake-like movement.

On clear calm days, the amount of area that is visible to the bass is greatly improved. It is also at this time that something called the mirror effect happens. Because the surface of the water has a different displacement value or surface tension, it has an effect of a mirror under water, helping the bass detect prey and predators.

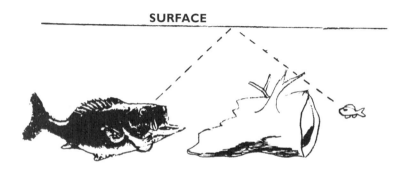

When fishing for shallow bass I believe it's important to dress in clothing that is camouflaged and avoid bright colors and shiny jewelry. The canoe I use also is camouflaged.

As you can see, the visual world of the largemouth bass is quite complex. As anglers, we should remember that we are an intruder into the bass' habitat and the less we make it aware of our presence, the better our prospects of a successful day. If we give the bass the opportunity to see a lure, we have at least taken one step inside the strike target.

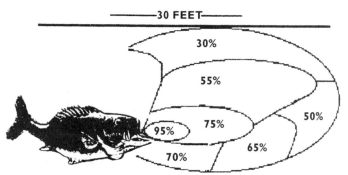

PERCENTAGE OF POSSIBLE STRIKE UPON VISUAL CONTACT

6. HEARING

S ound travels through the water much more rapidly than it does through air, and even though some of the auditory vibrations are absorbed by the water, the vibrations are able to travel great distances at close to five times greater speed than sound traveling through the air. Sound travels about 4,900 feet per second in water and about 1,130 feet per second in air.

Bass are able to distinguish audible vibrations between 18 to 1,000 hertz (hertz equals one vibration per second) with the best range between 250 to 750 hertz. The overall range for human hearing is much greater, starting at 20 hertz and peaking at about 20,000 hertz. The amount of vibrations (hertz) should not be confused with the volume of a particular noise, measured in decibels.

The human voice reaches an average of 25 decibels and, unless it is transferred through a dense object such as the bottom of a boat, almost all of the vibrations are unable to penetrate the water. If such a transfer were made, the amount of vibrations definitely would fall within the bass' hearing range. Here again, it is important to us as anglers to acknowledge the significance of positive and negative input when it comes down to largemouth bass behavior. Is a particular sound we're making presenting a food or flight situation for the bass?

I'm sure at one time or another most of us have experienced a noise that has scared us, especially if we were not expecting it. We can classify that description of a bass being scared by a noise as a sound disturbance.

At the other end of the spectrum, we have beneficial sound experience, which is a sound that may represent a gratifying experience and bring about a positive conditioned response. At this time, it will respond in a specific way based on past successful performances. And in the middle, alerting sounds induce the bass to select either a positive or negative reaction.

Most bass respond to sound in more or less the same manner. In areas where the sound of a boat is normal, bass are less likely to take flight and will assume that particular sound is of no concern. Bass establish sound zones, or zones of acceptance, that they can identify amid their surroundings. A sound coming from above a particular depth may draw a bass' attention but will not cause it to take evasive action. If that sound is coming from a depth where the

SURFACE

	ACCEPT
	ALERT
	FLIGHT

bass is not used to hearing it, the bass may take flight.

We've all heard the story of the angler out finding just the right spot to fish. When he finds it, he takes the anchor out and pitches it in the water, causing a big splash and making all kinds of noise. Actually, the big splash on top of the water may not spook the bass to move away, but it may alert him. If the bass is used to hearing splash sounds on top of the water, it may tolerate the noise as common and within the zone of acceptance.

On the other hand, once an anchor hits the bottom, making a noise within an area where the bass is not used to hearing a particular sound, the bass will most likely take flight. This is not to suggest that it is all right to fling your anchor overboard without concern. Remember, it may alert the bass to a possible negative situation.

In recent years, there has been a lot of discussion on lures that make some sort of sound. Are they good or bad? Here again, we find a lot of anglers giving the bass credit for incorporating total logic into its life. We have to break it down to much simpler forms of input. The bass is a predator fish and is turned on to feeding by many conditions of positive stimuli. It is seldom that just one particular stimuli is enough to elicit a strike-and-devour condition, but rather a series of events encourages the bass to strike. The noise from a lure may draw attention to the lure but, once that stimulus is observed, the bass most likely will need other incentives to continue.

Anatomically speaking, bass have inner ears (labyrinths) located on each side of the skull. They are missing the outer portion of the ear and for a few good reasons. By not having an outer ear, resistance within the water is cut back. A canal linking the outer ear with the inner could enhance the possibility of infection spreading to the bass' cranial organs.

Three semicircular canals are incorporated within the inner ear and help maintain a sense of balance. They are attached to a main structure called the utriculus. Off the utriculus are two other small structures called the sacculus and the lagena. Also located in the chambers are otoliths which are made up of minute particles of calcium carbonate called ear stones. Ear stones are used to estimate the age of fish since they show growth rings. The ear stones are joined to a group of sensory hair cells and work in conjunction with the sensory hair cells of the ampulla which are the gelatinous-filled enlargements at the end of the semicircular canals.

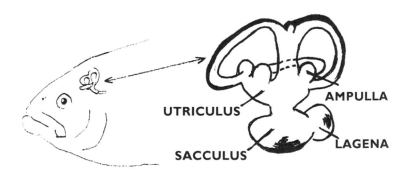

Whether the signals come from the ampulla or the otolith, they are carried to the brain by divisions of the auditory nerve. If sounds can trigger a bass into an aggressive posture, how do we know which sounds to use when it comes down to picking a particular lure? The truth is, we don't know how bass interpret sound. Is the sound broken down by the bass into a thought process, followed by response? Or is it just a reaction process? We can only speculate.

If we were to ask ten anglers which sound works best, we would most likely get a wide range of sounds, which should not be too surprising when we consider the audible range of the largemouth bass. The best rule of thumb is to consider the surrounding environment and to utilize sounds that may represent or closely resemble other noises that may exist there. Remember, the right sound may be just the thing to get the attention of a bass, but if it's going to strike, it may require you to entice its other senses.

In some fish, the Weberian ossicles (small bones that connect the swim bladder to the inner ear) play a role in detecting some vibrations. In the world of the largemouth bass, they have little significance, or at least have not been found to play a sufficient enough role to be examined in this writing.

7. LATERAL LINE

Largemouth bass are not unlike most other fish when it comes down to having sensory organs on the outer layers of the skin, better known as the lateral line. The lateral line is made up of numerous microscopic openings or pores located along each side of the bass, running from the head almost to the tail, and are able to detect low-frequency sound waves between four and about 200 cycles per second,

The receptor or cell unit that receives the stimuli is called the neuromast, which is located in the canal under the skin. The neuromast has two basic parts, the cupula and the sensory cells. The actual function of the lateral line is very complex but, in short, as water flows about the bass, the lateral line discharges a consistent stimuli at regular intervals. When this pattern is interrupted by a vibration within a particular cycle, the bass is able to determine if it is prey, an obstacle, or a predator. The larger lateral line nerves work to receive lower-end cycles, while the smaller nerves will receive higher-end cycles.

The location of the lateral line on the large-mouth bass also plays an important part of its overall function. The nerve sensors located up on the head of the bass will help determine local disturbances such as water currents, shoals, schools of other bass, prey and stationary objects. The lateral line located on the its side helps in sensing more distant disturbances.

Some experiments have been conducted on bass in which their sight has been blocked to determine if they could locate prey fish exclusively by utilizing their lateral line. After some time it was determined that they were able to shift more predatory sense responsibility to the lateral line, but because this particular experiment was done under a controlled environment, in a large tank with walls that confined any prey fish to a limited escape area. I personally have doubts that the bass would have had such a good success rate in an open habitat. Also, we do not know to what extent other sensory organs played in the role of the capture. The test did show the importance of the lateral line as a substantial part of a complex integrated network of senses in the bass' predatory world. As unique as the lateral line is, it does have its limitations and disadvantages when detecting smaller prey at longer distances. Larger fish are able to be detected by smaller prey fish first, since the lateral line is better at picking up larger fish at longer distances. This scenario also works to the bass' advantage when it finds itself the next possible meal for some larger predator, or there is a large school of prey fish giving off high doses of vibrations as a group.

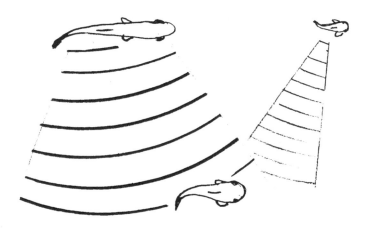

Of what importance is understanding the lateral line to the angler? If we remember the select functions of the lateral line as a sense able to feel distant pressure waves, we can fool that old bass into thinking that there is an easy meal for the taking. Injured fish or fish that are in distress give off lower and more erratic vibrations. Those vibrations are some of the best attention attractors known.

Remember, big bass do not like to chase healthy little fish. It's not energy-efficient for them, but if we use a large lure that has a slow methodical snake-like action, stopping every three to four feet and then giving it one or two quick jerks, we will have rung that big old bass' dinner bell.

I personally prefer the above method using seven- or eight-inch jointed top-water lures in shallow waters around mid-summer when water temperature is approximately 75 degrees. By using the larger jointed lures, we have utilized the bass' sense of distant touch at a time when it is most active or in its stage of primary growth potential, when feeding is at its zenith.

In spring, I prefer using smaller lures since bass are less active and seem to prefer the smaller and more vulnerable prey fish. Some of the factors that could play a part in why bass prefer smaller prey in spring may be better sight in colder waters than in warmer waters, less hiding places for the prey fish and smaller prey may help to facilitate the digestive processes (the digestive system of the largemouth bass will be covered in a later chapter).

The lateral line complements the hearing process by differentiating the lower-frequency sound waves or vibrations, but the point when hearing stops and the lateral line takes over is not that precise. There is an overlap of wavelengths by which both hearing and the lateral line are affected: those vibrations between 20 and 200.

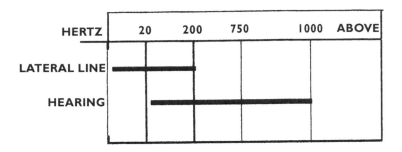

Hearing and lateral line senses supplement each other. Hearing will receive vibrations that may be coming from a distance that makes it hard for the bass to get an accurate locale of whatever is generating the vibration. Once the object is within the senses of the lateral line, the bass is able to localize the object's direction and visually make a food or flight determination.

If the bass has had prior experiences with a vibration, which it now recognizes as a possible threat, it doesn't need to authenticate it visually. It will move to a location that is less intimidating, generally not too far away, so it can return to its previous habitat.

We can best understand how the lateral line might feel to a bass by doing a small experiment on ourselves. First, place a small fan about six feet in front of yourself and sit on the floor with your arms folded in front (no sleeves). Then, with your eyes closed, have a friend take a stiff piece of cardboard (12" x 12") and move it in front of the fan at different distances and intervals. You should be able to feel the dissimilar air pressures. Even though this experiment is at best a poor example of what a bass feels through its lateral line, it does give us a small insight into the world of the largemouth bass. Hopefully, as time passes and we become more knowledge-able, experiments will reveal the bass' complex nature.

8. SMELL

Aromas are spread through waters much like they are spread through air, dispersed by means of currents or movements within the water. Unlike sound, scents that are in the water or are placed in the water take longer to diffuse than they do in air. As sound and hearing is to the lateral line, so it is with smell and taste. A bass will generally be able to smell and make a food or flight decision before it commits itself to tasting.

Because the largemouth bass is *stenophagous* (able to feed on few different types of food) its olfactory sense (ability to perceive smell) must be quite diversified, since it must learn to discriminate between thousands of odors in order to survive and propagate.

Many of the odors it will recognize are developed because of I.R.Ms, innate releasing mechanisms. As the bass becomes older, many chemical reactions take place that inspire it to perform certain tasks or to recognize new odors it may have never responded to before. Spawning is a good example of the I.R.M effect on the largemouth bass' ability to identify and react to a new, mature scent.

The bass can recognize many odors even at the earliest stages of development, while others are a slow-learning process. This trial-and-error process hopefully does not lead to its demise.

Just how sensitive bass are to scents is not fully understood, but their ability to discriminate various odors is quite impressive. Even as good as it may be, when ranking freshwater fish and their smelling capabilities, the bass would not be at the top of the list, but rather somewhere in the middle range.

Experiments have been done to see if there is a scent-related signal that helps the bass locate its haunts once it has been placed some distance from its known habitat. Some amazing results were recorded. Not only were the bass able find their way back, but they did so in a surprisingly short time.

Personally, I don't believe we can attribute such results just to the bass' olfactory senses. Other biological and sensory factors play a significant role in the bass' ability to find its way back to its habitat. Such things as the sun's location at a given time of day or even particular sounds could help with its trek. Most importantly, it will invariably seek out the best locality to persevere and, since it most likely has already found that spot before being displaced, it should not surprise us that it may randomly pick it again.

In previous chapters we have seen how different senses are able to overlap to bring about a response, a process called second-order conditioned reflex. Due to this conditioning, a response learned on the basis of the olfactory sense could be transferred to a visual response within time, just as an auditory response could also be transferred to visual response.

If we were to parallel the bass' second-order conditioned reflex to a situation that we can relate to, it would be something of the following nature. Picture coming home and smelling some homemade bread for the first time. You would not know what was giving off the scent, but, after some exploration, you would see that it was the bread creating the odor. Within a short time, you would be able to connect seeing the bread and know what fragrance to expect. One big difference here is going to be the bass' inability to learn the two associations as quickly as humans.

This would also explain why some largemouth bass react negatively if they come into contact with L-Serine (a chemical naturally produced by humans to which many animals respond adversely). Test have shown that L-Serine is not a natural substance of which largemouth bass are instinctively frightened, but rather a chemical to which bass may react negatively after routine exposure, most likely through catch-and-release.

There are some human products that contain odors that the bass may naturally find offensive because of its overwhelming power to have its olfactory sense distracted (much like if we were to smell ammonia). Some of the typical items to avoid touching before or while fishing would be: insect repellents, lotions, creams, perfumes/colognes or gasoline.

As in most teleost fish (spiny-ray groups such as perch, sunfish and bass), much of the anterior region of the brain, called the telencephalon, is devoted to the process of detecting and evaluating odors. Because so much of the brain is devoted to the sense of smell, we are able to see the importance Mother Nature has placed on the ability to detect odors in the bass' aquatic world.

BASS BRAIN

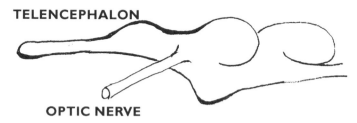

TELENCEPHALON

OPTIC NERVE

The nasal sacs on the bass are located on each side of its snout just in front of its eyes. These two small holes are generally referred to as nares. The nares consist of a bony capsule that contains the nasal sensory organs that is linked to the brain through the olfactory nerves. When irrigated with water, they are able to pick out a conglomeration of odors that the bass may recognize and determine an appropriate response.

As was stated before, largemouth bass have a moderately developed sense of smell which becomes more beneficial as they become older and experience new life situations, such as the development of the spawning odors, a process that may take three to four years in the northern largemouth bass and as little as one year in some of the southern varieties.

One question often asked is, "Do manufactured scents really work on bass?" My answer is yes, under certain conditions. We should remember that it takes time for a scent to circulate in water in order to be effective or to reach the olfactory receptors. Even if by chance we are lucky enough to have a water flow that happens to take the scent toward a bass, other sensory receptors such as sight or sound from a well-retrieved lure can trigger a strike response much faster. Personally, I prefer to use scents when I use plastic worms that may fall under close tactical scrutiny from a weary old bass, and as a taste enhancer so that the bass is more confident to keep the worm in its mouth once it is consumed.

9. TASTE

The sense of taste is the last hurdle that anglers may have to overcome in order to bring in that trophy bass. After all, it is at this point that the bass has used many of its other senses to get within devouring distance. Its next move is to come in contact with the object for the taste test. If your bait fails that final test, it may be no more than "the one that got away."

Taste buds in a largemouth bass operate mostly on the same principle as the olfactory senses, but to a lesser degree. The area where most of the taste buds are located is called the palatory organ, which is on the roof of the bass' mouth just behind the front teeth. Some taste buds can also be found on its lips. This is a rather convenient place to be, since any object it may wish to devour can be jettisoned very easily if found not palatable.

Unlike humans, who have about 9,000 taste buds, the bass has considerably less, since taste plays an elementary role when considered next to energy intake.

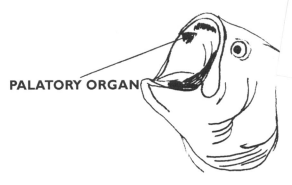

PALATORY ORGAN

Here again it is important to remember that the bass is stenophagous, and if taste were a primary factor in determining food, too much energy would be lost in the selective process. The full extent to which bass are able to discriminate taste is still unknown, but experiments have shown that they do have a priority or ranking when it comes to likes and dislikes, if given a choice, something that Mother Nature infrequently does.

Most experiments in this area are, once again, imperfect since they were done in a restricted environment, with selective foods. They did, however, prove that the taste buds are well attuned to anything that could be of harm or of no physical consequence to the bass.

There are many products that have entered the market that base their sales on the claim that, a particular component or hormone within their secret compound turns bass on when smelled or tasted. These seemingly magical compounds called pheromones are said to produce physiological activity within the bass, such as feeding. It has been my belief that such compounds, although well intended, are insignificant when considered to other overwhelming environmental factors that may elicit a strike-and-consume response. The bass is always under tant internal and external changes, and for e compound to convey such a heavy influence pon the bass that it would neglect all other senses is doubtful. This is not to say phero-mones don't fulfill a specific function.

What largemouth bass actually taste is purely hypothetical, but there is evidence suggesting there are taste buds that resemble those known to recognize such taste sensitivities as salt, bit-terness, sweet, and sour. It is also important to understand that each bass may have a taste preference. What may taste like food to one bass may be rejected by other bass in favor of more recognizable food taste.

Anglers who may wish to use taste enhanc-ers might do well to keep a variety of flavors and spices on hand, and don't be afraid to ex-periment.

10. TOUCH

When describing any of the senses it some-times becomes difficult to relate or trans-fer what a largemouth bass may feel in relation to what a human may feel or sense. The sense of touch falls within this gray area. We know that bass do have a small number of nerves within the skin that serve as receptors to touch when triggered by pressure, and that touch is involved in such behavioral patterns as spawn-ing or courtship. Is the contact or touch incon-sequential or does it serve as a stimulus to heighten a particular occasion? Experimenta-tion in this area suggests the latter. Touch may also serve as a temporary bonding between one particular partner or group of bass that are actively participating in a similar physiological occurrence.

One of the most useful applications of touch, and the one anglers should be aware of, is the bass' ability to discriminate between real food-stuffs and artificial ones in its mouth.

We all have heard some angler talk about the bass that spit out the lure before they had time to set the hook. Well, part of the problem could be the bass had time to differentiate between something to eat and something to reject, most likely because it did not feel right or natural in its mouth. Part of the problem here could also be that the bass was trying to turn the lure to make it easier to swallow or that it had a negative taste.

Because the exterior of a bass is so well in tune with its environment, mostly due to its reliance on the other senses, actual physical contact made to the epidermis (see Chapter 11) would be of little use as a sensory discriminator. Such contact may may even prove to be harmful by removing some of the protective slime (see Chapter 12).

From the angler's point of view, the primary concern should be about how the bass relates touch to feeding, especially since the bass' mouth does 98 percent of the total touching activity. It's also the angler's responsibility to keep sharp hooks just in case the largemouth decides to reject the lure. That way, there's at least a good chance that one of the hooks will become embedded even at the lightest touch.

11. SKIN & SCALES

The skin of a largemouth bass has two sections, an outer layer called the epidermis, and an inner layer called the dermis.

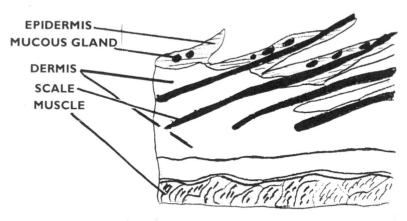

EPIDERMIS
MUCOUS GLAND
DERMIS
SCALE
MUSCLE

It has been said that one of the best comparisons of the epidermis of a bass' skin would be the inside of a human's mouth, since it is also composed of various layers of moist cells, the deepest of which aid in growth and cell replacement. As the newer cells force the older cells towards the outer portion of the bass' skin, older surface skin cells are removed by everyday activities. The epidermis also contains epithelial cells that carries a glue-like material that aid in closing any wound the bass may encounter.

The lower section of skin, or dermis, houses most of the functional systems such as the skin's sense organs, blood vessels, nerves, and connective tissue. The connective tissue can easily be seen by the angler when filleting a bass. The dermis also contains the coloring pigments called chromatophores, which gives the largemouth bass its distinct color and camouflage pattern. Furthermore, the dermis plays a significant role in the development and origin of one of the most recognizable aspects of almost any fish — its scales.

If you were to examine the scales of the largemouth bass, you would find two basic types. The first and most prominent would be the ctenoid scale, which has small comb-like ridges at its exposed end, and the other would look somewhat like the cycloid scale, which is a smooth disk-like circular scale that lacks the comb ridges.

The size of the bass' scales are in direct proportion to the amount of movement produced in any specific body region. Back by the very end of the bass' tail and around its cheek areas, the

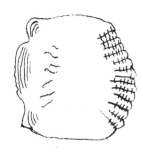

CENOID   CYCLOID

scales become much smaller because of the high percentage of movement involved there, while in the center of its body, where movement is limited, the scales are much larger.

Scales on a bass, as well as on other fish, are placed in an exact pattern on its body. This pattern helps to eliminate some of the friction caused by the scales when swimming. By making sure the scale drag factor is of equal proportions on each side, the bass will expend less energy in stabilization than if it were constantly trying to correct an unequal scale drag during swimming.

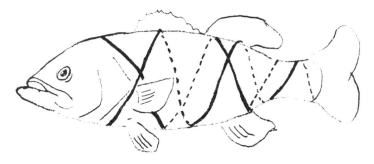

Not only do the scales provide an armor-like protection for the largemouth bass, but they can also provide us with some very important information about the bass' age. Almost undetectable to the naked eye, but visible even under the lowest-powered microscope, small rings within the scale can be observed. These rings are growth indicators since each ring generally represents one year of growth to the bass, and although the growth rings are an indication of the longevity of a particular bass, they by no means are an exact measurement, for within each scale there could be phantom rings that are caused by a shift in the bass' metabolism at any given time of the year. But, for the most part, this is an easy way for the angler to get an idea of the age and growth rate of the largemouth bass taken within any particular waters.

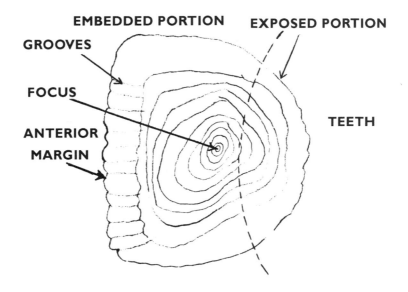

12. SLIME

For any angler, coming in contact with slime is just a way of life. You can't avoid its slipperiness or its pungent smell. It's something we, as anglers, take for granted, but to the large-mouth bass, it is a critical asset it cannot do without. Most fish produce slime but the quantity can vary a great deal depending on the species of fish, its habitat and the environmental conditions. The slime-eel, for example, is said to be able to produce enough slime to fill a large container in a short time. Fortunately for the bass angler, the largemouth bass falls somewhat in the middle when it comes to slime production. Slime is really a mucus that is produced in the outer layer of skin (epidermis) by tubular gland cells that extend to the outer surface of the skin. These cells have the capability of covering the bass with the slippery mucus.

The purpose of these conjugated proteins (slime) are multiple in function for the bass. It helps smooth out the surface of the skin to create less drag for the bass as it moves through

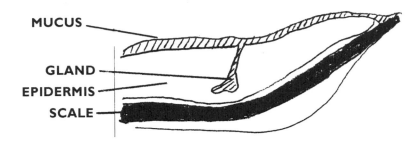

the water. Slime may also function as a chemical communicator through the olfactory system, alerting bass to physical or biological changes.

One of the most important functions of slime is in the prevention of infections that could locate on the skin or be transmitted through the skin. Since slime is always being produced, the outermost surface of mucus is constantly being sloughed off throughout the bass' daily activities. Because of this natural purification process any organisms or irritants are eliminated.

One of the most vulnerable times for a largemouth bass to lose its slime protection is after it has been caught and handled by the angler. To eliminate some of the possibility of slime removal, handle the bass by holding it firmly with your thumb just inside its lower lip and your first finger under its jaw, and try not to remove the bass completely out of the water.

What may be the thrill of a lifetime for an angler may be a catastrophic event for the bass when caught. If you plan on releasing the bass, remember all the negative physiological things that your bass may have encountered.

When a bass is caught, there's an increase in lactic acid from strenuous muscle activity. This leads to an increase in its respiration, by which some of its natural body salts are lost, and a large proportion of its energy reserves are depleted. If the bass came from deep water, residual air may occupy the air bladder. The list could go on and on. Even though the angler may not have much control over the internal complications of being caught, there is one factor we do have control of, and that's how we handle the bass when it is in our possession.

It is the angler's responsibility to provide the best possible environment to the bass in order to increase the chances of its survival. When possible, release the bass in the water from where it came and do so in a timely fashion. If you're using a live well, make sure it is well oxygenated, cooled (if possible) and use additives for slime and salt protection.

13. CIRCULATION & BLOOD

The circulatory system of the largemouth bass is very distinct in its performance, in that, blood that is relatively high in carbon dioxide is passed through the gills where it is once again replenished with oxygen. The amount of blood volume in the bass' body is considerably small, only accounting for about two and a half to three percent of its total body weight. (Humans have up to six percent total body weight in blood.)

The bass' blood, as in most fish, consists of a fluid called plasma that has blood cells known as erythrocytes, or red blood cells, which contain an iron compound called hemoglobin that helps transport the all-important oxygen throughout the bass' body and into the leukocytes, or white blood cells. Of all the different types of leukocytes, two stand out. The first, called a thrombocyte, is involved with blood clotting and makes up about half of all leukocytes. The second is called a lymphocyte, that produces antibodies to help combat infections and diseases.

Location can make a difference in the bass' antibodies, as the requirements of certain antibodies can differ from lake to lake, although it seems to be a more regional difference than a local one.

The absorption and utilization of salt is very important to the life of a bass. The blood is relatively rich in salts when compared with the waters in which the bass lives.

The largemouth bass' heart is located behind the gills just in back of the lower jaw, and just in front of the pelvic fins. Because of the low

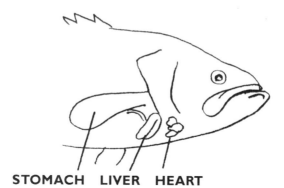

STOMACH LIVER HEART

blood volume, the bass' heart size is relatively small when compared to the overall size of the bass, and will stay in close weight proportion throughout its life.

Even though the heart is small, the location may be the bass' own shortcoming. It's the heart's location with which anglers must be most concerned. Hooks that are set too deep, in the far back of the throat, have the potential of penetrating into the heart.

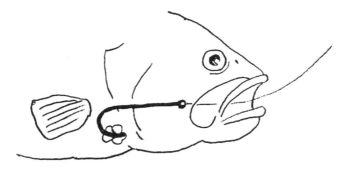

When penetration of the heart happens, you will generally see blood coming from the gills, and little of the shaft of the hook exposed from the throat. If you plan on releasing the fish, don't remove the hook. Cut the shaft of the hook as far back as you can without additional injury to the bass and release it back into the water as quickly as possible, since water helps the clotting process.

If the bass is to survive, the best chance for it is back in its own natural environment, even though the odds of surviving such a injury are minimal. If the bass does not respond or death seems apparent, make the best out of a bad situation and enjoy some bass steaks. Check codes for size limits.

14. RESPIRATION & GASES

One critical need of the largemouth bass, not unlike other animals, is the need of a sufficient supply of oxygen in order to sustain life. The problem here is that water is not the best medium to hold oxygen consistently enough throughout its total mass to make life easier for the bass. If we were to compare equal amounts of water and air, we would see that air holds about 35 times more oxygen than water, and since water is about 800 times more dense that air, extracting the much-needed oxygen from the water must be done in a highly effective manner. A largemouth bass gathers oxygen by moving water over its gills, where millions of red blood cells containing hemoglobin are able to isolate the oxygen from the water. It is then carried to various parts of its body to aid in the conversion of energy from fats, sugars, and other nutrients.

The problem with the above circumstance is that oxygen is very inconsistent in its amount

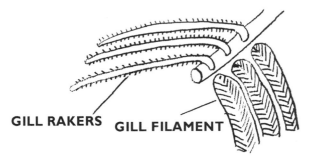

GILL RAKERS GILL FILAMENT

in any given proportion or body of water.

The amount of breathing motions done by the bass is related to its size, age, activity and concentration of oxygen. If a bass were to find itself in a very low-oxygen situation, its respiration would not only quicken, but the depth or volume at which it must breathe could increase as much as four times. If the bass were not able to improve its shortage of oxygen, it could find itself in a circular definition, whereby it would be working harder to get more oxygen but consuming or using more than it can take in, which would ultimately lead to its death. This is a good reason to keep live wells properly aerated. Generally, the oxygen level would have to fall below four parts per million (ppm) before any critical oxygen deficits would occur. Because the bass' blood is able to hold about 20 times more oxygen when compared to the same volume of water, the oxygen consumption rate does not depend on the oxygen concentration rate within the water until it reaches the critical oxygen deficit.

It is important to note that the rate of oxygen consumption becomes lower because of the relationship between oxygen use and the body weight of the bass. This could account for seeing some larger bass in areas which we might consider somewhat stagnant. But we should remember that bass do not have a crystal ball to determine that when moving to a new area that they may stumble into a lower oxygen environment.

Oxygen deficits in any given body of water can be produced by a variety of factors. One that we may see every time we go fishing is phytoplankton, microscopic plants that give the water its green appearance. These plants are two-faced in nature, giving off oxygen during sunlight hours and using up oxygen during the dark hours, also known as bloom.

Another form of oxygen depletion can be found in the process of decomposition. In waters where there is a great deal of matter in the process decomposing, you will most likely find a build-up of noxious gases such as hydrogen sulfide and methane that replace oxygen and are deadly for the bass. As an angler, you should be able to recognize the smell of methane and hydrogen sulfide since they have been compared to the odor of rotten eggs or sewer gas. If you do come across a place that is eliciting such an odor, chances are bass have be forced to move to a better area.

Water temperature also can have an affect on oxygen consumption. As water temperature

increases, the amount of oxygen used by the bass will also increase, because its tissues demand for more oxygen increases, which seems to go against the bass' odds for survival since warmer water holds less oxygen. In reality, even when the water temperature reaches into the nineties, there is still enough oxygen for the bass to survive easily.

Another gas that we should recognize is carbon dioxide (CO_2). Increases in carbon dioxide can lead to a decrease in the use of oxygen by the bass. Here again, the bass may find itself in a circular definition, and in jeopardy of its own demise if unable to change its situation. Carbon dioxide can be displaced in water much easier than oxygen, and, in one sense, this is good for the bass because it helps eliminate carbon dioxide from its body through the gills as a by-product of body waste. On the other hand, if it is not kept under control, especially at the human waste level, we could see a marked decrease in bass populations.

Oxygen is introduced into waters by means of diffusion from the air and photosynthesis from plants, when carbon dioxide is taken in by the plants and converted into oxygen. It should be very clear to us, as anglers, the importance that aquatic plants play in the lives of the largemouth bass. Consequently, largemouth bass like to spend time around plants that are very active in the photosynthesis process. Such plants are easy to detect because of the dark green color they exhibit. (See Chapter 20).

The oxygen-gathering parts of a bass are a tightly packed series of thin plates, which have a series of branch-like projections. Because of its design, the plates present a great amount of surface area for water to pass through, enabling more oxygen to be absorbed. It is interesting to note that the bass gills are so efficient that they are able to pick up about 80 percent of the total oxygen that passes through them, but if there is a shortage of this life-giving gas in its environment, it won't matter how efficient the gills are.

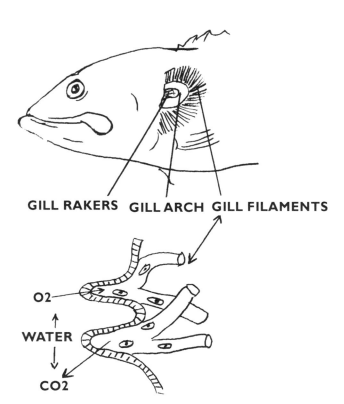

GILL RAKERS   GILL ARCH   GILL FILAMENTS

O2

WATER

CO2

15. FOOD & NUTRITION

Some of the more popular theories about what largemouth bass eat have been put to careful examination in the past few years, only to find that the bass will eat or at least try to eat almost anything if it appears as a possible food source.

Fortunately, the largemouth bass has adapted to a broad variety of foods over its thousands of years of existence, thus its sensory organs and physical qualities complement it in every way. Because of the way it hunts or gathers food, it is easy to see why we classify the largemouth bass as a predator fish.

The bass' feeding behavior is not as cut-and-dried as we would like to believe. Most anglers never stop to think about the bass' ability, and at times inability, to adapt to a feed-and-consume situation. However, understanding what may be available for the bass to eat at any given time, combined with the right presentation, can have a positive result in your catch ratio. It is important for us to understand that not only does the quantity of food play a significant role in the bass' life, but the quality of the accumulated foods are critical to its survival. Some foods it may consume will have more beneficial effects on its development, while other foods will be limited in their supportive role in its everyday survival. It is highly unlikely that bass understand this concept of selective nutrition and actively seek out foods that meet a higher nutritional criteria, but rather rely on availability and ease of capture when selecting their meal.

As the largemouth bass becomes older, the foodstuffs it consumes will also change or shift with its nutritional needs and capturing capabilities. A small fingerling bass of one-to-two inches will start out by eating zooplankton and small underwater insects. By the time it has reached three-to-six inches, it will be seeking larger insects and small minnows as well as other small life forms. At twelve inches or more, its diet is thoroughly diversified and has adapted to whatever prey is within its surrounding environment.

As the bass enters advanced adulthood (about eighteen inches or about eight years in southern Wisconsin) it once again changes its predatory habits. Bass in this advanced stage of life may favor prey that is 15-to-25 percent of its body size, preferring less chase and resorting to smaller, less alert prey. A smaller bass may try to consume prey 40-to-50 percent its size. While taking advantage of smaller prey seems to be its primary objective, larger prey on occasions may present an easy target without the expense of much energy, such as when a fish is injured or in distress or just plain forgets it could become a meal and wanders too close.

Another favorite target of mature bass is the

highly vulnerable and exceptionally nutritious crayfish. Bass that are fortunate to have a large population of crayfish that crawl within the rocky shorelines of their waters will experience superior growth rates over bass that feed on other typical prey.

Growth rates of largemouth bass vary greatly because of the type of food consumed, ranges of temperature and ability to convert useful foods into energy. The conversion of food to growth can be measured by knowing the bass' weight and then, over a given time, comparing the new weight to the old. Unfortunately, to do an accurate conversion we need to know the total weight of food consumed during that time, something most anglers do not know. Below is a chart of the average growth rate for a southern Wisconsin largemouth bass. Please note that the graph is based on an average growth rate, and that all lakes may differ to a greater or lesser extent.

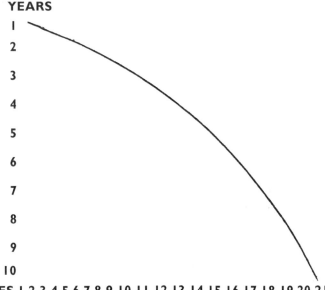

YEARS

INCHES 1 2 3 4 5 6 7 8 9 10 11 12 13 14 15 16 17 18 19 20 21

As the left-hand part of the graph indicates, the older a bass turns, the slower its growth rate becomes. This is due to two distinct factors. The bass simply lowers its food intake, due to the fact that more energy is used at the locomotive or physical level than at the growth level. Secondly, it is less efficient at converting the food elements (protein and carbohydrates) into usable growth potential, that is, tissue and bone growth, with some energy being used to converted foodstuffs to the fat reserve. Thus, the larger bass may only be able to chemically convert about fifteen to twenty percent of the usable food elements into growth, whereas a younger bass may be able to convert about 40-to-45 percent.

Although a bass can go for long times without food, it is obviously best that it doesn't, for the longer it waits, the less efficient its digestive system becomes. Even though it may start to eat again it will take some time before the bass returns to its original digestive productivity, excluding starvation situations. During the low digestive state, the bass also is more vulnerable to disease and infections.

Food consumption is also closely related to the health conditions of the bass. A bass that is in poor health will instinctively slow down so more energy may be directed to the injury or infection. Once again, it is important that we remember that the largemouth bass is stenophagous, in that, it must expend less energy in capturing food.

In order for the largemouth to stay healthy, it must at least consume about 1.5 percent of its total weight per day in foodstuffs, and in order to grow at any reasonable rate its total intake must reach at least two-to-three percent of its total weight. It is not limited to those particular percentages, rather only to the size of its stomach and its ability to digest the food at a reasonable rate.

The growth rate is also influenced by the presence or lack of vitamins in the food. Growth rate is greatly reduced if there is a shortage of the vitamin B in its diet, but can quickly be restored if placed back into the bass' diet. Thus, even bass within the same age group in a particular lake may experience growth retardation because of the lack of even concentrations of vitamins. (More on digestion and the effects of temperature can be found in Chapter 16.)

1. Top bass is a normal bass at 2 years with a length of 8.7 inches and a weight of .38 lbs.

2. Middle bass is 7 years old with less vitamin intake and weighs 1.2 lbs. at 12.6 inches.

3. Lower bass is also 7 years old with a length of 16.8 inches and a weight of 3 lbs.

16. BASS &
TEMPERATURE

I t is clear, even to the novice bass angler, that water temperature plays a critical role in the everyday existence of the largemouth bass. Anglers who sincerely understand the concept of temperature and bass behavior have a definite advantage. Because the bass is a cold-blooded creature, the temperature of the water surrounding the bass has enormous significance to its metabolic rate. Within the bass' body, the temperature will differ only by one-half-to-one degree higher than the water around it, and in many cases will be the signaling component for a natural stimulant to induce a particular behavior (IRM).

In nature, no doubt, there are many controlling factors that involve feeding behaviors. Temperature is one factor that forces adjustments in the bass' daily feeding characteristics. The ideal feeding and growth temperature for the largemouth bass is between 75 and 90 degrees, with the mean being about 80 degrees. As the water temperature drops, the rate of feeding starts to decline until about forty-five degrees, at which it has reached a point that the bass have all but stopped feeding.

Digestion of foodstuffs is also affected by the temperature. At about 80 degrees, the bass' digestive capabilities are at their best, taking only about 20 hours or less to complete. At about 60 degrees, it has slowed down to the point of taking about 55 hours and at 50 degrees or lower, it will slow down to about five or more days.

The sense of temperature by the bass is not unlike many of its other senses in that when a particular change in the bass' environment takes place, it is received by the sensory nerves, in this case, by the free-nerve endings in the skin. This change is transmitted to the brain where it is interpreted and followed with a reaction. The amount of temperature it takes in order for the bass to recognize a change is very small and may be a little as 0.05 degrees.

The metabolic rate or activity level of the bass increases as the water temperature rises. This increase has a direct effect on how an angler may want to choose the size of the lure and the speed at which it is retrieved. With a rise in temperature, the bass' possible growth potential has increased and its level of feeding activity must also increase to meet all of the nutritional demands now placed on it. This aspect of higher metabolism has been called Van't Hoff's Law, which states that for every 20 degrees of rise in water temperature, the bass' activity level rises by 300 percent.

In the northern areas like Wisconsin, the decrease of the metabolism has a direct effect on the life span of the largemouth bass. In southern waters, bass may occasionally live up to 10 years while northern bass can reach the ripe old age of 14 or 15 years. The average age is closer to 9 years for the female and 6 to 7 years for the male bass. It's interesting to note that the average Wisconsin largemouth bass outlive most Wisconsin white-tailed deer.

The diagram below is based on averages and could vary depending on lake and location. It is also based on larger trophy size bass.

TEMP.	DEPTH	LURE SIZE	PRESENTATION (SPEED)
90	0 to 3'	med.-large	very slow, jerky, fish in distress, snake-like, worms of no weight
	3' to 5'	med.-large	slow-to-medium speed, jerky, distress, worms of no weight
	5'+	med.-large	medium, mild jerk, up-down, worms with little weight
85	0 to 3'	med.-large	very slow, jerky, fish in distress, snake-like worms of no weight
	3' to 5'	med.-large	slow to medium speed, jerky, distress, worms of no weight
	5'+	med.-large	medium, mild jerk up-down, worms with little weight
80	0 to 3'	med.-large	very slow, jerky, fish in distress, snake-like worms of no weight
	3' to 5'	med.-large	slow to medium, jerky, distress, worms of no weight
	5'+	med.-large	medium, mild jerk, up-down, worms with little weight

TEMP.	DEPTH	LURE SIZE	PRESENTATION (SPEED)
75	0 to 3'	medium	very slow, jerky, distress, snake-like, worms of no weight
	3' to 5'	medium	slow to medium, jerky distress
	5'+	medium	medium, mild jerk, up-down, worms with weight
70	0 to 3'	medium	slow, jerky, snake-like worms of no weight
	3' to 5'	medium	slow, jerky, snake-like worms with little weight
	5'+	medium	slow, mild jerk, up-down, worms with little weight
65	0-3'	medium	slow-to-medium slow worms no weight
	3' to 5'	medium	slow, jerky, snake-like worms little weight
	5'+	medium	slow, mild jerk, up-down, worms with little weight
60	0 to 3'	small	very slow, mild jerk worms of no weight
	3' to 5'	small	slow, mild jerk, up-down, worms of no weight
	5'+	small	slow, mild jerk, up-down, worms with little weight
55	0 to 3'	small	very slow, mild jerk worms no weight
	3' to 5'	small	very slow, mild jerk, up-down, worms of no weight
	5'+	small	very slow, mild jerk, up-down, worms with little weight
50	0 to 5'	small	very slow, mild jerk up-down, worms with little weight
	5'+	small	very slow, mild jerk, up-down, worms with little weight
45	5'+	small	very slow, up-down worms of no weight

This diagram should be used as a guideline, since all lakes differ from one another and may have temperature variations at different times. Within any given body of water, sudden temperature changes may cause shock and possible death but, for the most part, largemouth bass have learned to cope with such matters.

Lakes that the largemouth bass inhabit in the northern region, such as Wisconsin, are called temperate lakes. These are lakes in which the surface temperatures can range above or below four degrees Celsius or about 40 degrees Fahrenheit. Within these lakes, temperature stratifications occur at different levels of water. Because of these temperature levels, the movements by the largemouth bass may be restricted.

In the summer, when the sun is able to warm the top layer of water faster than the winds can mix it with the other strata, we are able to locate three distinct strata: the top layer called the epilimnion, the warmest of the three and possibly the area of highest bass activity in the summer months; the thermocline, which is the middle layer; and the hypolimnion, which is not only the lowest and coldest of the stratifications, but likely carries the least amount of oxygen.

As fall approaches, the largemouth bass must once again adapt to a possible temperature and

WATER SURFACE	
EPILIMNION	65-75°F
THERMOCLINE	45-65°F
HYPOLIMNION	39.2-45°F

THE DENSITY OF WATER IS GREATEST AT 39.2 DEGREES FAHRENHEIT. WATER BECOMES LESS DENSE AS IT WARMS OR COOLS BEFORE FREEZING (32 DEGREES F).

area change, since the waters will now be going through what is known as the fall turnover. In fall, there is a decrease in air temperature and a shortening of the daylight hours which, in turn, lower the epilimnion water temperature. There is also an increase in winds that will mix or homogenize much of the top strata. Largemouth bass at this time may be found anywhere in the lake but are inclined to locate in areas that are experiencing less severe change.

Water is unique in its reaction of declining temperatures, in that, as the temperature of the top stratum reaches about 39 degrees F. (3.9 degrees C.), it begins to sink because it has reached its highest density, taking along with it much of the oxygen found there. Unlike other liquids, once it has cooled down to around 32 degrees F., it becomes lighter and stays at the surface, where it freezes, leaving the warmer water deeper. The ice layer will provide some additional insulation, and if the ice is clear enough, it will let some plants continue to furnish the much-needed oxygen. But there also is a threat of plants decaying and using up vital oxygen. This process is called winter stagnation and is one of the most critical times that the northern largemouth bass must face each year. I've seen entire bass populations in some of the shallower lakes die out because of such harsh conditions. Aerators placed in critical areas can reduce such conditions.

The temperature of the water, as any angler can perceive, has considerable significance in the life of the largemouth bass, and can play an important role in the changes of its food spectrum, since all of its natural prey also must live within the same temperate conditions (see Chapter 19). Any feeding activity, area movements or food-supply source will be affected in one way or another by increases or decreases in the temperature, which is going to be a major factor for the angler to consider at all times.

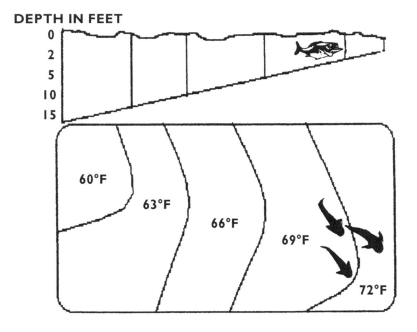

17. SPAWNING

R eproduction in the life of an adult large-mouth bass is a cycle that assures the continuation of its species. Bass have adapted three particular relationships that help it to follow through with that primary function: behavior, physical conditions, and seasonal periods. These all serve as influences to the species in order for it to fulfill responsibilities of spawning.

Skillful anglers have learned to adjust to these seasonal changes, and use them to their advantage. Each stage of the cycle is preparing the bass for the next transitional period, which is ultimately controlled by environmental factors.

Spawning first starts out with seasonal changes in the sun's movement, the moon's gravitational pull, and other changing environmental factors to bring about a natural course of migration for the bass. About that same time, the water temperature rises to about 55 degrees F., when the adult male largemouth bass first receives a chemical message (I.R.M.) telling it to move into shallow water where the temperatures are uniformly higher.

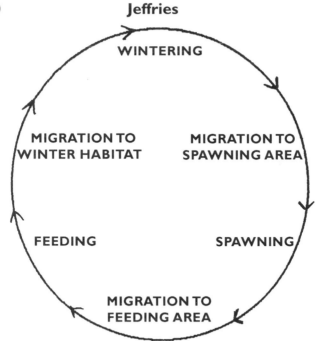

The adult female bass has been building up an egg supply inside her eggsac during the past few months. The number of eggs can vary a great deal depending on the age of the bass, but is generally thought to increase with age until she approaches advanced adulthood where it may start to decrease. Unlike her male counterpart, the female largemouth bass is less willing to move quite so willingly into the shallows.

Once the water temperature has reached about 60 degrees F., the male largemouth has completed building or sweeping away an area approximately two-to-three feet in diameter by about five-to-eight inches deep. Sand or gravel in about 18 inches of water is preferable, but he will select other coarse bottom material if sand or gravel is not available, and may choose a little greater depth if other areas are ill-suited. The largemouth bass also likes its seclusion, and will build the nest 30-to-40 feet from other nests when possible.

By the time the male is done building the nest he has become very aggressive and is determined to seduce an eligible female into his nest. The female likely will be larger in size than the male. The larger and often older female bass are inclined to spawn earlier than younger and smaller females. The fact that the larger of the females spawn first is not just a coincidence, for it is the larger females that contain the most eggs, about 5,000 per pound, and will deposit them early in the spawning season when the male's milt is the most potent, assuring the highest percentage of fertilized eggs.

As a female nears the prepared nest, the male may try to bite or snap at her side or tail, possibly to sense by either taste or smell if she is available. If she is persistent in her approach, she will eventually enter the nest tilted to one side with her head facing down. The male, then assured of her intent, will swim to her side and move to the bottom of the nest. With their caudal fins close together, she will deposit the matured eggs. The soft, light-yellow eggs are sticky and adhere to the stones, weeds or other brush in the deposit zone. The male then deposits his milt, eventually fanning the area with his tail, to make sure the milt has spread throughout the eggs to ensure a high percentage of fertilization.

She may not deposit all of her eggs in one nest but may choose to move on until more eggs have matured and are ready to be deposited. The male may not be content with one attempt at one fertilization, and may actively seek another female, even though his milt becomes less potent with each encounter.

Much of the spawning process takes place

during the early evening hours, just before significant darkness sets in. At this time of evening, the waters are generally going through a wind or weather-shift transition. In other words, the winds have died down, the turbulence in the shallows has reduced and all is still. This is a time of day I call the witching hours, referring back to my Vietnam days. It also gives the bass some protection against predators that visually feed, since visibility is greatly reduced.

The spawning process can take up to four weeks or more before the female bass is rid of the mature eggs. Any other immature eggs will be absorbed back into her system. Once the female is done, she will retreat to an area where she is most comfortable and recuperate from the physically demanding ordeal. The male, on the other hand, will stay at the nesting location to deter any strangers that may wish to have the newly fertilized eggs as a main course. He will endure this protective kinship with his newly formed family until his I.R.M.s switch him back to a eat-or-consume mode, at which time the new bass fingerlings may learn their first lesson in predator-prey correlation and be eaten by their sire.

The fertilized eggs need a large amount of oxygen in order to develop correctly, and any lack or low oxygen levels will terminate any future development. Any decomposition taking place within the immediate area could jeopardize the development process. To help eliminate that possibility, the male bass fans the nesting area circulating fresh oxygen to replace any harmful gases that may develop. The fanning also helps to decrease the possibility of fungal infections to the developing eggs.

The eggs start to develop rapidly, going

through various stages as the water temperature rises. Within three-to-eight days, newly hatched bass or fry will emerge. In about a week, the yoke sac is absorbed and the fry must rely on micro foods.

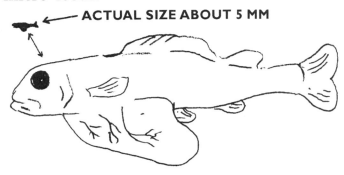

ACTUAL SIZE ABOUT 5 MM

They may remain within the nest up to a month, while the male bass guards them most of the time. Once they reach fingerling size, the now miniature bass leave the nest, joining with other fingerlings from the neighboring nests to form schools. Unfortunately for many, this journey outside of the nest will be their last, for a very low percentage ever make it through the next two-to-three years, becoming victims to those that may themselves eventually be consumed by the bass that survived.

Assembling into schools will decrease as the bass become older; by the time they become young adults they may be in schools of as little as five to 10 bass, with many of the senior bass preferring to be unaccompanied, living a life of solitude. As you can see, the spawning period is an excellent time to catch large bass in the shallows, but being a responsible angler during this time is essential. Releasing the bass with as little stress as possible, or using barbless hooks can help place that trophy where it belongs — at the nest.

18. BASS & pH

pH is a measure of both alkalinity and acidity. The higher the pH level reading, the greater the alkalinity. Just the opposite is true for the acidity, since lower level readings mean more acid is present. In pure water, neither acid or alkaline, the water is said to be a neutral solution, which has a pH factor of seven.

If we look at the pH indicator below, we will see that the acid levels on this particular instrument start out at four and graduate to seven

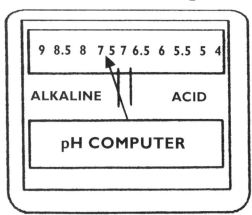

minus; alkaline starts out at seven plus and extends to nine.

In the past few years we have seen or heard about the significance of acids in the lakes or waters. We should be quite concerned, and with some justification, about the consequences on bass populations from acids. This is a serious problem, the total effects or possible damage of which are still unknown. The difficulty in determining the overall damage to the largemouth bass as a species stems primarily from the variances in the lake's or water's degree of hardness or softwater effects.

A bass living in a lake that is considered to be a hard-water lake will be affected less by acid than a bass that is living in a lake considered to be a soft-water lake. This can be explained by the fact that hard water has concentrations of carbonate salt of calcium and magnesium that act as a buffer, which helps protect the bass from the acid's influence.

In soft water, which is for the most part not buffered, acids are able to do the most damage to the bass. The damaging effects are of a twofold concern, since the acid will break down the gill arrangement, causing respiratory complications, which lead to a respiratory circular definition. The second concern is possible damage to the bass' intestinal wall, which could affect digestion and cause internal bleeding.

The amount of damage done generally depends on the amount of time spent in an undesirable area, and if adequate conditions for recuperation exist. Healing may take place with some aftereffects such as weight loss, open sores, eye damage and other less visible injuries.

Temperature will also have an effect on how much harm is done to the bass. In lower temperatures, the bass' metabolism is slowed and less acid is distributed internally, reducing the overall detrimental dosage. This does not mean bass won't pass through areas of less acceptable pH levels.

Injury to the bass occurs in levels that go beyond 9.5 (alkaline readings) and 5.5 or below (acidity readings), preferred pH levels from 7.5 to 7.9 with an overall tolerance range of 6.7 to 8.3.

HEALTH RANGE TABLE FOR pH LEVELS

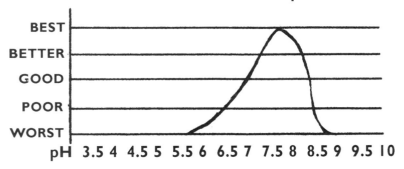

BEST	
BETTER	
GOOD	
POOR	
WORST	

pH 3.5 4 4.5 5 5.5 6 6.5 7 7.5 8 8.5 9 9.5 10

LEVELS OF HARDNESS MEASURED IN PPM
OF CARBONATE OF SALT OF CALCIUM

WATER	(CaCO3)
EXTREMELY SOFT	0-9
VERY SOFT	10-39
SOFT	40-159
HARD	160-279
VERY HARD	280-399
EXTREMELY HARD	400

It must be noted that pH levels can be higher or lower within the realm of hardness, that is, water that is extremely soft with a ppm of (CaCO3) at 0-9 can still have a pH level of eight, which could suggest a possible high level of algae bloom. A pH level of 3.0 to 5.0 with a ppm of 40-159 can not only indicate acid input, but suggest the presents of carbon dioxide (CO2) toxicity.

It is also interesting to note that the pH of slime is the same level as the preferred level of pH (7.5-7.9) for water, thus helping to stabilize the slime for a more effective and efficient system for the largemouth bass.

The pH level is also a critical element when it comes to the development of eggs. Too much acidity or too much alkaline can have catastrophic effects on the developing bass eggs.

Acids that enter the water have many diverse resources that help in producing possible damaging effects, many of which we may not think about. We have a tendency to fault the large factories, with good cause in some cases, for destroying or adding to the disastrous effects of acids, but in reality we are the ones responsible for a large percentage of the damage.

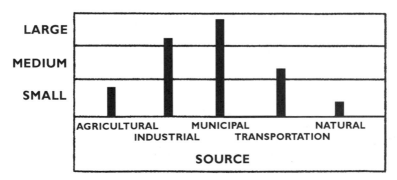

There are different types of acids that have potential side effects on the life of the bass, each with a greater or lesser effect depending on its toxic capabilities.

ACIDS' TOXIC INFLUENCE
(ranked by most potent)

1. tannic	5. benzoic
2. chromic	6. acetic
3. sulfuric	7. citric
4. hydrochloric	8. lactic

NOTE: More can be found on bass kills in Chapter 22.

From the angler's point of view, we should remember that pH levels can range not only in depth, but can vary at equal levels around the body of water in which we're fishing. Dark green vegetation is generally a good indicator if you do not have access to a pH meter.

19. NATURAL BASS PREY

In the world of the largemouth bass, it truly comes down to a matter of survival. It's just that simple, or is it? To the angler, food is something that we can just go out and buy or catch, prepare, and consume. We are, for the most part, able to choose what we eat, where we eat, and how much we eat, primarily because we have a choice. We have the ability to select, make decisions, and carry out a plan using logic, with an idea of what the consequences of our decisions will be.

Largemouth bass, on the other hand, are very fundamental when it comes down to food selection and consumption. They are by no means an epicure, at least by human standards. However, by bass standards they do rather well. The actions or responses of bass towards food derive from instincts or learned condition responses which develop around the available food resources, an important aspect for the angler to consider when selecting baits for a particular

area.

The range or variety of prey can be vast, with each lake, pond or river exhibiting numerous species of prey for the largemouth bass. Largemouth bass have even been observed following birds and aquatic animals to snatch any prey that may have been forced to abandon their hiding place. Once pressured into the open, the prey find themselves an easy meal ticket for the bass.

It would be difficult to cover all of the possible prey with which a largemouth bass may come into contact. Therefore, we will cover a few of the more typical ones on the following pages.

Recognizing the basic potential prey within an area is a must for the serious largemouth bass angler. We can classify or group the possible selection, eliminating a lot of guesswork. Remember that within any body of water there are seven major groups or selections of prey: crayfish, salamander, frogs, snakes, worms, insects and other fish. Each prey has a particular time or season in which it may become more active. Knowing these times may help the angler

to establish criteria for lure selection and presentation.

THE CRAYFISH

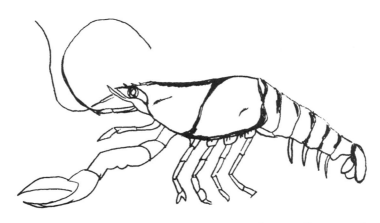

A very popular discussion that often arises
at my seminars is on the crayfish. I'm often told
by many anglers that one of their favorite presentations is one that imitates the crayfish. My
response is, "Which one?" Wisconsin has a re-
ported nine or more species of crayfish that be
long to the *Cambaridae* family.

For this particular writing we will discuss
one of the most common and widespread Wisconsin crayfish, the *Orconectes (Gremicambarus)
virilis*. In general, crayfish are found in steams,
rivers, lakes, and occasionally in small pools,
ponds, and small streams. As to specific locations, it is able to live in a very diverse habitat,
including aquatic vegetation, shallow water ex-
cavations beneath stones, and burrows in shore
banks, and leaves small mud mounds, or chim-
neys, as a sign of its presence.

Crayfish can tolerate pH levels of 5.5 to 9.5
but prefer levels of six-to-7.5, and temperatures
of 41-to-92 degrees (5-to-33 degrees C.). Males seem

to be able to tolerate warmer waters, while the female of the species prefers colder waters. This could account for the smaller size of females, since their metabolism is slowed down.

During daylight hours, crayfish remain in their burrows or under rocks and become active just after dusk. Individual crayfish seldom move to a new area. If the population becomes too intense, they may move quite some distance to relieve the pressure. In areas where conditions are suitable, there can be up to a 1,000 lbs. per acre or about 8,000 crayfish. Since the crayfish is a scavenger, it will feed on virtually any organic material.

Female crayfish, generally starting in their second year of life, lay eggs in early spring, often in mid-April, around the shore region where food and shelter are more accessible and the water conditions are more suitable for the egg developing process.

After egg-laying, the female will generally stay around for a while, but after the eggs hatch, often in June, she will migrate to deeper waters. The male, however, stays in shallow waters through the warmer months.

ACTIVE TIMES

THE SALAMANDER

In general, there are many types of salamanders that inhabit a vast amount of area, but they all have one thing in common — the need for water. Agricultural and city growth haven't seemed to bother most of the populations and because of the high numbers around bass areas, they have become a favorite imitation lure for the angler.

Salamanders are, for the most part, burrowing creatures, but become active above ground between mid-March and mid-April during the heavy warm rains, at which time they may seek breeding waters. Once at the waters, courtship begins, egg laying and fertilization take place at the bottom, where the loose egg mass is attached to some form of vegetation.

In two to three weeks, the larvae appear and, by the end of August and into early September, the well-developed young adults are ready to migrate out of the waters, which is once again done during warm rains and usually at night. The average size of a salamander is five-to-six inches but it can reach 14 plus inches.

THE NEWT

Many anglers confuse the newt with the typical salamander, and justly so. It actually belongs to the salamander family but has a very different life style. The newt is predominantly an aquatic critter and will inhabit some waters during the course of its entire life. Unlike its salamander cousin, the newt may stay active all year long and has been seen under ice on some lakes and steams.

Courtship and mating take place during late fall and winter with the actual egg-laying taking place around April. Adult newts are active throughout the day and can be found crawling along the bottom of shallow waters, using the vegetation as a foothold as they travel. Once spooked, they may swim rapidly for safety, with legs tucked by their sides and using their tails as paddles.

As to coloration, the newt is of a light brownish color on its back and has a light yellow underside. Small pepper-like spots can be found over most of its body.

When newts leave the water and inhabit the land, they then are called efts, which are said to have a very strong and foul taste and are left alone by many of their land predators. The newt has a average size of two-to-three inches.

THE MUD PUPPY

The mud puppy, unlike the newt, has large red branch-like gills that enable it to stay submerged on lake bottoms and around shorelines. Like the newt, the mud puppy is also active throughout the year. In clear waters, it is nocturnal, but in stained waters it may be active throughout the day. In late October, you can expect to see them gathering in rather large numbers to mate in the shallow waters, with a preference for rocky shores.

The females are nest builders, constructing the nest in late spring, usually late May or June, when they will stay with the eggs for a period of about two months, guarding and fanning them.

I often have encountered mud puppies late at night, when they seem to be attracted to the lights from my boat. I also remember my Grandmother Daisy taking me down by the old mill dam to pick up mud puppies so we could cut off the tails and fry them up for supper, a delicacy I consider right up there with one of my favorites, squirrel tongue.

The mud puppy's color is of a darker brown with a light gray speckling and dark spots. The average size is seven-to-eight inches but they can grow up to 14 inches plus.

THE FROG

There is a large number of frogs here in the north. Some of the most common are the bull frog, green, leopard, pickerel, and the tree frog. For this book, we will cover one of the most common — the green frog.

The green frog lives in almost all ponds, lakes and other waters in Wisconsin and stays close to the water's edge throughout the warmer months, when they mate in the summertime waters they consider home. Young green frogs migrate long distances from fields in order to get to water where mating usually happens at night. Mating calls that start about mid-April can be heard throughout the day. Much of the egg-laying activity occurs in May but egg-laying can take place much later.

The males are very aggressive during the early summer months and vigorously defend the shallows they consider their territory. When they are threatened, their best defense is to plunge to the bottom and wait for the danger to move on but they must come up for air and it is during this time that they are most vulnerable to the largemouth bass.

Frogs in general stay very active when water temperature is between 70 and 90 degrees. They also like to live where insect populations are in great abundance. One of the best times to use a lure that simulates the frog is, unfortunately, one of the worst times for the angler — late at night in a bug-infested area close to shore.

One of the best largemouth bass fishing days I have experienced was due to the presence of a very large bullfrog that Paul and I came upon while fishing out of my canoe one day. Paul and I had spotted him jumping around in an area that was heavily grown-over with algae. Because of the particular disturbance it was creating, largemouth bass were trying their best to capture it but were unsuccessful because of its overwhelming size. Seeing this, we went over and started casting worms down the holes the bass had just made while trying to get the bullfrog. Each time, Paul and I came up with a five-to-eight pound bass, which isn't too bad for Wisconsin largemouth.

THE WATER SNAKE

The northern water snake, as one can derive from its name, is found around water and is fair game if located by any large bass. It can grow up to a length of 40 inches but is generally seen when about 15 to 25 inches. The color is gray with reddish-brown bands outlined in black.

Water snakes come out of their winter hibernation about mid-April and, after some adjustment, start mating in May. The newborn snakes, which can range in numbers from 12 to 45, emerge from the mother already hatched (ovoviviparous). The young can be born from August to around the middle of September.

Most people confuse the water snake with the water moccasin, but the water snake is non-poisonous. In fact, I have yet to see snakes that inhabit the Wisconsin waters that are poisonous.

Lures that imitate the snake-like action are some of the best bass enticements I have found. Water snakes seem to be an easy target for waiting bass and bring out the aggressive nature in the largemouth bass.

The active time for water snakes is from April to mid-October with primary activity on those days when the temperature is above 80 degrees. If you see this harmless creature, leave it alone. Its bite can leave a nasty wound. Bring out the lures that best fit its snake-like action. Fish the shallows around logs or rocks that may be sticking out of the water or in and about lily pads. Remember that one of the snake's favorite foods is the green frog. Get the picture?

EARTHWORMS

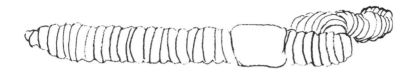

As anglers we all must have at one time or another used earthworms for a variety of fish and it seems to be a fact that fish, including the largemouth bass, savor worms.

Earthworms can be defined as secular invertebrates which contain or have both male and female parts but are not self-fertilizing (hermaphroditc). The eggs that are produced are cocoon-like and, when fully developed, bear an offspring that looks very much like the adult earthworm.

Since earthworms are land or subsurface creatures, how is it that fish seem to be so confident in consuming them? Simple. Many earthworms meet their demise in waters occupied by bass by entering the waters involuntarily, either by rainwash or flooding over low lands.

Earthworms generally live within about a foot of the surface but will move deeper during adverse conditions or periods. At certain times, environmental conditions dictate that they move to the surface. It is at these times that the worm is obviously the most vulnerable (about mid-March to May).

Early spring rains that bring on days or nights of thunder and rain that saturate the soil will move worms to the surface, especially at night. Check the pavement at sunrise outside your house. If it is littered with worms, consider calling in sick and hitting the shores. Shores that are very fertile and have good clear runoff may be the first to consider, or banks that are cement or rock-lined where worms may have gathered are good too. Water that is murky from runoff may have an adverse effect on largemouth bass and they may elect to move to an area that is more suitable for overall survival.

Check the pH levels before and after rains at specific locations on your lakes or ponds, and also at different levels to determine the influences of runoff. By eliminating or reducing locations that may have low bass populations due to unfavorable runoff, you may be able to increase your bass-per-hour ratio. Worms prefer soil that has a pH level of seven.

If you're using actual nightcrawlers, a double hook with a center worm harness may be preferable. I choose not to use a worm weight with this rig in order to have a more natural action.

Most anglers are very aware of the seasonal changes around them but fail to observe changes within a given body of water and how those changes affect fish in general, especially smaller fish like bluegill. (More on the effects of weather and largemouth bass are discussed in Chapter 21). Smaller fish are one of the prime indicators of feeding and habitable areas. Before any fish can be consumed by the largemouth bass, it must first and foremost meet the seasonal rhythms of a feeding largemouth bass and be available within the daily intervals of feeding.

A good fish prey indicator for largemouth bass can be done by simply observing the shallows and making note of the various types of fish along with their color and swimming patterns. Remember that a largemouth bass can consume a fish about half its size, so don't be afraid to use large musky lures in good bass waters.

Because largemouth bass have the capacity to learn through repeated events (conditioning), not all prey fish may meet the older and wiser bass' criteria. Therefore, use your lure in conditions and areas where it would pose an easy meal, remembering that largemouth bass favor targets above them, instinctively aware that most prey fish do not see objects very well below themselves.

Some of the common types of prey fish are the shad, bluegill, sunfish, and minnow. Each one of these fish may present a different tactical skill that must be learned by the bass in order to be successful in capturing a particular prey fish.

BASS & INSECTS

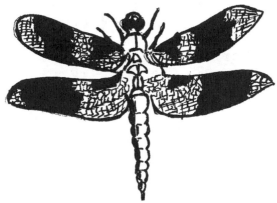

It would be nearly impossible to cover all of the insects that may inhabit ponds, lakes or, for that matter, any water system. Insects are by far the largest group of animals, larger than all of the other groups of animals combined. All insects belong to the class *Insecta*, also called *Hexapoda* (six-legged). There should be no mistake about the role they play and its importance in the everyday cycle of life in and around bass waters.

Even though insects can make for a good in-between-meals morsel, larger bass generally wait for more substantial prey, unless large quantities of insects are available. But insects do play a key role in the development of a younger bass and make up a large portion of its diet, at least until the bass can move up in its dietary selection.

Aquatic insect larvae, particularly those of the mayfly, dragonfly, caddis-fly, etc., make up the highest percentage of insect prey in the waters. Other substantial amounts of insects are ingested by bass when the insects fall into the water from shore or as aerial insects pass within striking distance.

INSECT ACTIVITY LEVELS

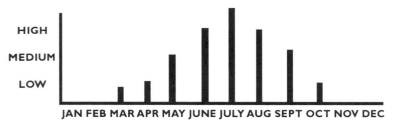

Since insects are part of the predator/prey cycle, their location can give the angler a good idea of where fish may be active and, in turn, where bass may be actively hunting those fish.

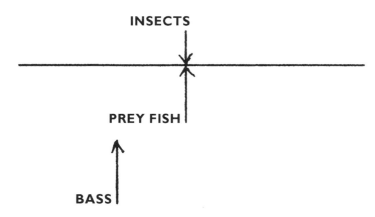

A great way for some fast action on an ultra-lite is to capture a large dragonfly, hook it through its head using a fairly small hook, gently cast it by a lily pad edge and retrieve it using small short soft jerks.

20. LARGEMOUTH BASS & AQUATIC PLANTS

Plants and largemouth bass go hand in hand and the significance of plants in the life of a bass cannot be overstated. Although vegetation may be a pain when you are constantly removing it from your hooks, the large bass often hold out in the weeds.

Aquatic plants can be divided into two basic groups: microscopic, which are one cell plants such as fungi and algae; and larger multiple-cell plants called macroscopic.

Although most plants are beneficial for the bass, fungi can harm the fish by developing in wounds and destroying tissue, which can possibly lead to death.

Algae, commonly called scum or slop, is another one-cell plant that is a familiar sight to the largemouth bass angler. When fishing in slop, be ready for some heavy action. I have found that I have the best success when I use imitation worms (no weights) and hit the inside holes. On windy days, bass seem to hold up on the wind side of these holes. Casting the worm to the other side and letting it float gently down, twitching it as you retrieve, will produce some great results.

Chlorophyll-bearing, or macroscopic, plants, are enormously beneficial to the bass, as they provide oxygen, hiding places or a place to rest during inactive times. Some of the more notice-able plants are the water lily, milfoil, curly-leaf cabbage, coontail, and bulrushes.

These larger types of plants can be divided in to four groups, each lending its own unique design to the bass' habitat:

1) free-floating plants that exist on or be-neath the surface.

2) floating-leaved plants with roots attached to the bottom and leaves floating on the surface.

3) submerged plants that are usually rooted with stems and leaves below the surface.

4) emergent aquatics that are rooted in water but have stems with or without leaves that ex-tend out of the water.

As bass anglers, when we first approach a particular weed we should first ask ourselves, "Why would a bass be here?" and secondly, "What type of prey inhabits this variety of weed?" Par-ticular plants consistently draw certain types of prey, an uncomplicated theory most anglers fail to realize.

Recognizing that each plant will have differ-ent growth habits at different stages of the year will help you to establish what I call the 3-P prey strategy: plant, prey and presentation.

Plants that establish themselves early in the year will naturally attract fish or other prey to them for primary spring grouping. Along with grouping, fish seek out specialized plants that establish basic nutritional needs, protection and reproductive sights. As the season progresses, more plants develop, giving the prey a more diverse selection, which in turn spreads them over a larger area. As the season ends, some plants will hang in there until ice is formed. Areas with late-period plants are great for fall fishing.

There is one major rule that I try to practice when fishing near aquatic plants. In order to be a good productive bass area, there should be a good entrance and exit zone for the bass to utilize. In order to help us visualize this concept, let us look at the white-tailed deer, since they also use this particular strategy. Think of the entrance and exit area as a tree line that connects two separate wooded areas. The deer will move back and forth between the two woods much more readily if it is able to use the tree line as a passage way.

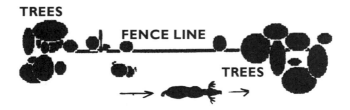

Another good feature to look for when fishing near aquatic plants is a variety of weeds grouped in a particular area. Bass will relate to those areas since they have the potential of having diversity of prey and because dissimilar plants root themselves to different types of bottom soil, which may provide alternative routes to other food areas.

LILY PADS (floating-leaved plant)

Water lilies generally grow close to shore in about one-to-four feet of water. They may provide good spawning sights if the bottom is not loaded with a substantial amount of mud or decaying material. During the early spring, largemouth bass may hold out around lily pad areas, partly because the water conditions that are favorable for lily pads to grow also are beneficial for the seasonal shift of other fish that bass can feed on.

In mid-to-late summer, the pads become much more dense, at times looking thick enough to walk on. But don't let the dense top fool you. There is generally ample room below for even the biggest of basses. Larger bass take advantage of this summer feeding bonanza and concentrate in and around the pads. Shallow, interior pockets provide an excellent opportunity for a trophy bass.

One of my favorite methods when fishing near lily pads is to look for what I call runways. This is an imaginary line that will give you a clear run through the pads. In doing so, you are able to use larger floating lures of about three-to-four inches that have a higher hook count for better catch percentages. Using a slow stop-and-start retrieval with a light jerking action works best. This is also an area where I seldom use worm weights when using artificial worms.

Largemouth will generally hold out around pads until water temperatures become cold enough that you can notice considerable color and structural changes in the pads. At that time, try deeper pad edges mixed with other plants.

MILFOIL (submerged plant)

Milfoil can become very dense, almost to the point that bass are unable to maneuver through it. In some areas it has become a problem weed, choking out other vegetation.

Smaller fish like to hide in and around this plant because of its high density. If the plant becomes too widespread, bluegill and other prey fish become stunted, leaving predator fish unable to move about in its thick mass to capture the overpopulated fish.

Since milfoil grows in large clusters, it will generally have well-defined edges and an occasional good interior pocket where bass can congregate. Look for an overlap of other weeds and concentrate on those areas. Using shallow-to-medium diving lures along the edges is best. It's also a good area to use live bait. Artificial worms with a small weight could produce a nice bass from the interior holes. Milfoil is one of the last weeds to hold out before ice-over.

CURLY-LEAF CABBAGE (submerged plant)

Cabbage usually is found in about five-to-eight feet of water and may indicate a drop-off point on the front edge. It is usually distributed in such a way that you are able to fish its small-to-medium pockets by weedless jigging or artificial worms with weights. Another good presentation is to use shallow running lures up and over its submerged stalks. The deep edges provide some good action, as long as northerns are not around, and are great cover for late fall bass. It, too, is one of the last plants to survive before ice-over.

COONTAIL (submerged plant)

Coontails have always been a good bass areas for me, especially when they are of a dark-green color. You can generally find these plants anywhere from three-to-eight feet of water, where they may reach the surface in the shallows and remain as submerged clumps in deeper waters, extending only about three-to-four feet off the bottom.

Locating a single patch of coontails at mid-depth, or about five feet of water, and that is on the edge of a cabbage or milfoil area can yield the angler some nice bass. In this particular situation, I prefer a weightless artificial worm placed in an open area right next to the coontail, and let it float gently down while softly twitching it.

BULRUSHES (emergent aquatics)

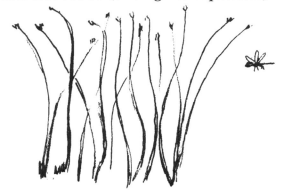

Bulrushes, or reeds, are disappearing from our shores at an alarming rate. In the past, I remember when most lakes had large pockets of these bass magnets surrounding the entire lake. Unfortunately, they are becoming harder to find, which is not only detrimental for the anglers and bass, but unfortunate for the lake water, since bulrushes help to eliminate many unwanted chemicals.

Bulrushes grow in areas where the bottom is mostly sand. These areas are considered excellent bass spawning grounds as well as great largemouth bass haunts. In my travels, I'm surprised at how many bass anglers have not tried bulrush areas or have not had the opportunity to try them.

As late-spring plants, bulrushes generally become infested with bass just as the tips of the plants begin to show through the surface. They provide excellent bass fishing throughout the summer and early fall days. As the old saying goes: *When bugs leave the reeds in haste, bass will soon seek another place.*

When fishing this particular weed, I prefer to use what I call aerial casting, which is simply tossing a artificial worm with a small weight as high as you can at an inside hole. Your line will then come down parallel with the reeds, letting the worm reach the water in deep pockets. Most anglers try to toss their worm horizontal to the weeds, which will almost always get the worm hung-up.

We have only covered a few of the weeds, but it should give you a good idea what to look for and how to follow through with your own presentations when fishing in weedy areas.

21. BASS & WEATHER

There are few situations that an angler may find him- or herself in that can be more frustrating than weather changes, simply because we have no control over them. They can ruin the best made plans or they can make for a dream-come-true fishing experience. Nevertheless, they are something we can overcome mentally, if not physically.

Weather changes are a process in which bass develop various cycles or patterns of behavior; weather conditions link all species together down to the smallest of living animals. The specific peculiarities of each animal will have a direct effect on its next principal prey link.

We can divide the behavioral conditions as related to weather and largemouth bass into three stages:

1) *Transitional stage:* The stage at which bass are physically adjusting to favorable or unfavorable activity conditions, primarily due to I.R.M.

2) *Full acclimation stage:* The stage at which bass have physically made their adjustment to the changing environmental factors and are re-

acting accordingly.

3) *Conclusion stage:* The stage at which bass have completed a particular behavior or set of specific behaviors and are reverting to the transitional stage.

Each length of a particular stage is dependent on the magnitude and consistency of any one weather condition. The exact time a bass may change its physical activity because of atmospheric conditions is still unknown, but there are indicators that may help anglers predict a reasonable activity or behavioral change. We first should look at understanding specific conditions and how they may relate to bass.

Air masses or pressure systems are constantly moving around the earth's surface, meeting with other air masses. The borders of where these elements meet are called fronts. High-pressure systems are generally identified with cold fronts and move or rotate in a clockwise direction. Low-pressure systems move counter clockwise and are generally identified with warmer air.

Because cold air is heavier than warm air, it will exert a downward pressure on the earth. When this happens, the pressure rises on the earth's surface. Just the opposite can be said of a warm air system, as it will lighten the pressure. To measure these two occurrences, we use a barometer.

Most anglers own a barometer but seldom use it correctly because just reading it will only confirm what the weather is in his or her particular area at the present time. In order to help the angler to determine a possible weather change, the barometer should be used in conjunction with the current wind direction. The following wind-barometer table is from the official U.S. Coast Guard Boating Guide.

WIND-BAROMETER TABLES

WIND	BAROMETER	POSSIBLE WEATHER
SW to NW	30.10 to 30.20 steady	Fair with temperature changes in 1 or 2 days.
SW to NW	30.10 to 30.20 rising rapidly	Fair, followed within 2 days by rain.
SW to NW	30.20 & above stationary	Continued fair with no large temperature change.
SW to NW	30.20 & above falling slowly	Slowly rising temperature and fair for 2 days.
S to SE	30.10 to 30.20 falling slowly	Rain within 24 hours.
S to SE	30. 10 to 30.20 falling rapidly	Wind increasing with rain in 12 to 24 hours.
SE to NE	30.10 to 30.20 falling slowly	Rain in 12 to 18 hours.
SE to NE	30.10 to 30.20 falling rapidly	Increasing wind, rain within 12 hours.
E to NE	30.10 & above falling slowly	In summer, with light winds, rain may not fall for several days, in winter rain or snow in 24 hours.
E to NE	30.10 & above falling fast	In summer, rain within 12 hours. In winter, rain, snow, increasing winds.
SE to NE	30.00 or below falling fast	Rain will continue 1 or 2 days.
SE to NE	30.00 or below falling fast	Rain with high wind, followed within 36 hours by clearing, and in winter by cold.
S to SW	30.00 or below rising slowly	Clearing in a few hours, fair for several days.
S to E	29.80 or below falling fast	Severe storm imminent, followed in 24 hours by clearing and, in winter, cold.
E to N	29.80 falling rapidly	Severe NE gale and heavy rain, in winter, heavy snow & cold.
W	29.80 or below rising fast	Clearing & colder.

On days where you see a drop in the barometric pressure you should expect to see an increase in bass activity. Generally, the faster the pressure changes, the faster the bass' activity levels also change.

Low-pressure systems that travel from west to east bring storms, which lower barometric pressure since winds circulate counter-clockwise and bring southern warm air. This accounts for the old saying;

When the wind is in the west,
The fishing will be at its best.

Be careful not to let those nice, westward, warm southern breezes fool you. What may start out to be a great fishing trip with some great fishing experiences may end up as a total washout. It's important to get to know the signs of weather changes if you want to become a fishing guide. It's best to be honest with your clients about the approaching weather so you and they can plan accordingly.

When air masses that have different temperatures meet, they do not mix well and create fronts. There are three types of fronts — cold, warm and occluded — each affecting bass, or should we say, giving bass the opportunity to respond differently. Let's take a look at each one of these fronts and consider its potential effects on the largemouth bass.

Cold air is somewhat unstable and therefore very active, generally moving at speeds of 20 to 35 miles per hour and, for the most part, emerges from the north or northwest.

COLD FRONT

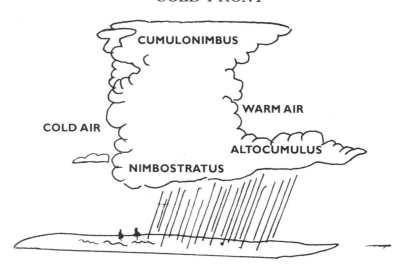

As the cold front moves in, it pushes under the warm air and, as the warm air cools, heavy rains can occur sometimes with very little warning. Most of the time you will see an increase in the barometric pressure as the cold front approaches, with gusty winds from the north or northwest. During this time, bass will slow down their activities since much of their prey has moved and their energy can be conserved until better opportunities and probability for capture become available.

Don't let cold fronts discourage you. Larger bass are less affected by the appearance of a cold front and are often the last fish to move out. Try fishing deeper drop-offs with a very slow retrieve.

There are times when the barometric pressure can fall during a cold front, as when there is an incoming storm from the northeast. This type of storm usually has little effect on temperature changes. A cold front with a lowering of the barometric pressure can have a positive effect on bass activity. Nimbostratus and cumulostratus clouds are usually associated with cold fronts.

WARM FRONT

Warm air is somewhat more stable than cold air, and will move relatively slowly through an area, usually at about five-to-20 miles an hour. The approach of a warm front is usually easier to predict since warm fronts generally have a typical cloud sequence as they approach, which, in order of their appearance, are cirrus, cirrostratus, altostratus, and nimbostratus.

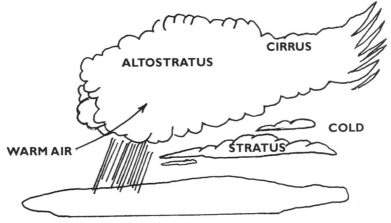

Rain from a warm front may last for several days, which often is called a stalled front by anglers. An incoming storm from a warm front will most likely have winds moving out of the southeast or northeast with increasing temperatures. The barometric pressure falls steadily, which generally makes for excellent bass activity.

An outgoing storm from a warm front typically has a leveling effect on the barometric pressure with winds coming more from the south or northwest. You will commonly find bass in any of the three basic activity levels during these times: active, impartial, and idle.

OCCLUDED FRONT

An occluded front happens when one air mass is trapped between two other air masses. What happens next depends on the temperatures of the three air masses. Violent thunderstorms or tornadoes are a result of this type of front with a very visible cloud mass forming as high as 75,000 feet. Because of the severe conditions that could be involved with this particular weather front, anglers would be at great risk to venture out under such circumstances.

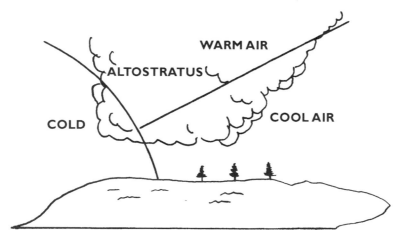

At times you will encounter winds that seem to be working against you, but remember, large-mouth bass react to almost every weather condition with the same conditioned response. Food gathering and survival are their primary objectives. They will try to accomplish those tasks with as little expended energy as possible. Work with the wind, remembering that the smallest of foods, such as zooplankton, will involuntarily move with the wind, building up food walls or stacks against banks, reeds, or any wall that interferes with the wind. Once the buildup is at a sufficient size, smaller fish will take advantage of the intensified feeding condition. Bass from the local area will then follow suit and actively feed.

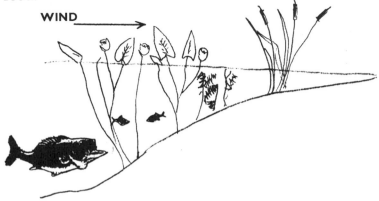

We can't always be around places where we have access to the local weather station but, never fear, for Mother Nature has provided us with a little insight into the oncoming weather by allowing us to observe signs in nature that are for the most part reliable. Listed below are some of the forecasting signs that may help to establish bass activity.

(1) Strong coffee will hold bubbles at the outside edge of your cup during a low pressure system and hold bubbles in the center of your cup in a high-pressure system. I personally like this one since it gives you a chance to forecast first thing in the morning.

(2) Frogs will increase their singing a few

hours before a storm shows up.

(3) A halo around the moon could be a sign that rain is on the way.

(4) Dew early in the morning or late at night is generally a sign of continued good weather.

(5) A sky colored dark red, yellow, green, or blue-gray could mean rain and winds.

(6) Birds that tend to stay on a fence or phone lines may mean a low barometric pressure.

(7) Mosquitoes feed heaviest about 12 hours before a storm and stop just before it arrives.

(8) Often the smell of new mown hay will linger in the air as a storm approaches.

(9) Sound will travel further as a storm approaches.

(10) Smoke will stay lower to the ground during a low pressure system. If it rises in a high vertical column, you can expect fair weather.

(11) Red sky at night, the weather probably will be clear the next day. Red sky in the morning means you will most likely receive a storm during that day.

(12) When the dogwood blooms, the bass will hit soon.

As anglers, we should remember that Mother Nature may wish to change our environmental conditions any time she wishes so be ready to give way and bow to her needs.

MOON PHASE

There has been much discussion on the effects the moon has on fish. Personally, I don't pay much attention to it. Although it may play a small part in the activity levels of fish, I don't believe its influence is justification to fish any harder or any easier than at any other particular time.

The activity levels of insects and other smaller prey does seem to rise somewhat during full moon phases. This occurrence could indeed account for a higher activity levels in bass. But to say you landed more bass just because of a full moon could be inaccurate. You may be selling yourself short and maybe you're just using some good angling skills at those particular times.

22. MAN'S INFLUENCE ON BASS

E nvironmental evidence associated with man's potential destruction of largemouth bass is well documented. As easy as it would be to point an accusing finger at the next person, we all contribute to a greater or lesser degree in the depletion of beneficial bass habitat. One of the most critical sources of bass kills has been diagnosed as toxicosis, or chemical poisoning.

The list below may help you recognize clinical signs associated with toxicosis as listed by the U.S. Department of the Interior.

SIGN	POSSIBLE CAUSATIVE AGENT
White film on gills, skin, & mouth	Acids, heavy metals, trinitrophenols.
Sloughing of gill epithelium	Copper, zinc, lead, ammonia, detergent, quinoline.
Clogged gills	Turbidity, ferric hydroxide
Bright red gills	Cyanide.
Dark gills	Phenol naphthalene, nitrate hydrogen sulfide, low oxygen.

SIGN	POSSIBLE CAUSATIVE AGENT
Hemorrhagic gills	Detergents.
Distended opercles	Phenol, cresols, ammonia, cyanide.
Blue stomach	Molybdenum.
Pectoral fins moved to extreme forward position	Organophosphates, carbamates.
Gas bubbles (fins, eyes, skin, etc.)	Supersaturation of gases.

The clinical signs listed above must be observed in a freshly dead bass, since the signs disappear soon after its death.

In bass kills caused by toxic substances, it's generally the smaller bass that are killed off first. But when there is a depletion of oxygen, larger bass seem to be the most affected.

The rate at which bass die can be a helpful tool in finding out the cause. If large numbers of bass die abruptly within 24 hours, it is often due to a overwhelming consequence in which a toxic agent has been introduced into its environment. If the mortality rate occurs over an extended time, such as five-to-seven days, the cause of death may mean that there is a pattern of oxygen depletion going on, which is the most common natural cause of bass deaths.

Even though we associate oxygen-depletion kills mostly with winter, summer oxygen depletion deaths do occur. Heavy rains following a long hot spell in summer can create a summer turnover, which may bring about anoxic water (water with little oxygen) that may send the bass into an oxygen deficit.

As a young boy, I remember going on camp-outs with my father in which we would often set up camp next to a lake. At many of the lakes we would not only be able to fish, but were able to use the water fresh out of the lake for drinking and cooking, a practice nowadays I would hesitate to do. Currently, only about two percent of the total water on earth is drinkable.

GLOSSARY

Aerial casting: Lofting a lure high in the air so the line trails the lure coming down, which helps keep the line from getting hung up on the bulrushes.

Alerting sound: The period during which a sound has a warning effect on a bass.

Beneficial sound experience: The period during which a sound has an attracting or favorable effect on bass.

Carangiform locomotion: A movement that gives a side-to-side alternating wave which helps to propel a fish.

Carbonate salt of calcium: (CaCO3) Chemicals that when present in water help to make up hard water, which acts as a buffer against acids.

Circular definition: A pattern in which one or more factors causes a reaction, that eventually reverts back to the original circumstance, which leads to a repeated cycle.

Conjugated proteins: Proteins that connect, forming a thick mucous membrane called slime on a fish.

Ctenoid scale: A particular external plate-like structure forming the covering on bass.

Decibel: A unit used to express relative acoustic power.

Epidermis: The outer layer of skin just under the scales.

Fingerling: A small or minnow-size juvenile bass.

Hermaphrodite: Having both male and female sex characteristics.

Hertz: A unit of frequency equal to one cycle per second.

I.R.M. (Innate Releasing Mechanism): Natural chemicals in fish that, when released, cause a specific behavior.

Isocercal: A caudal fin that is of equal size or proportions on both top and bottom.

L-Serine: A chemical produced by animals thought to have a negative effect on other animals.

Lateral line: A group of specialized nerves located in the outer layer of skin of fish and which are able to detect vibrations.

Littoral zone: That area of water that is associated with shallows or zones close to the shore.

Magnesium: A chemical that when present in water, assists in acting as a buffer against acids.

Mesotrophic: A type of very fertile lake that hosts a variety of species and supports a large range of vegetation.

Nares: Two small openings on the snout of fish that circulate water and allow the fish to detect objects.

Offensive lunge posture: A position held by a bass just before it sprints forward towards its prey.

Ovoviviparous: The capability of hatching eggs internally, giving birth to live young.

Pheromones: Chemicals released by some animals that cause a specific reaction in other animals.

Phytoplankton: Microscopic plants that are able to give off oxygen during daylight hours, but use oxygen at night, also called bloom.

Primary growth potential: A point in the seasonal change when food is very abundant, lending to a very good overall growth rate.

Pivotal drag: A fin extended out in such a manner that it causes a resistance to that side of the fish, thus forcing a turn.

Rule of survival: The ability to exist within or outside of a particular group.

Runway: An imaginary path through lily pads that enables the angler to retrieve a lure without snagging.

Side flex rotation: A side-rotation movement made by fish, generally at the surface, that enables it to return to deeper water.

Second-order conditional reflex: A response brought on by repeated events that are identified by one particular sense that will eventually be recognized by other senses.

Stenophagous: Able to consume a few different food stuffs.

Surface tension: A high density sheathing effect on the surface of water that acts like a clear skin-like coating.

Telencephalon: The large portion of brain in fish devoted to the sense of smell.

Teleost: Spiny-ray groups of fish such as perch, bass, and sunfish.

Temperate lakes: Lakes that are susceptible to seasonal change.

Weberian ossicles: Small bones associated with the air bladder that assist some fish in hearing.

Van't Hoff's Law: For every 20 degrees of water temperature increase, bass metabolism will increase 300 percent.

Witching hours: The early evening hours when

it becomes calm and still.

Zones of acceptance: A sound or noise that a bass is used to hearing at a particular depth.

Zooplankton: A microscopic animal that is a source of food for small freshwater fish.

BASS GUIDES SHORE LUNCH

4 nice bass fillets
2 strips bacon
1/3 stick butter
1 medium onion
3 tsp lemon juice
2 tsp liquid smoke
seasoning salt
garlic power
black pepper

Using a large frying pan over medium heat, fry up bacon taking it out when it is done. Leave fat in the pan, mix in butter, lemon juice, and liquid smoke. Place bass fillets in pan and season to taste with spices, cover with chopped onions. Place a tight lid on top of pan and cook until bass fillets flake. No need to turn the fillets over. Mix in fried bacon and leftover chopped onions in fried potatoes as a side dish.